Kintyre and South Argyll

40 walks in Knapdale, Gigha, Bute and the Cowal Coast

The author and publisher have made every effort to ensure that the information in this publication is accurate, and accept no responsibility whatsoever for any loss, injury or inconvenience experienced by any person or persons whilst using this book.

published by
pocket mountains ltd
The Old Church, Annanside,
Moffat DG10 9HB

ISBN: 978-1-907025-952

Text and photography copyright © Douglas Milne 2023

The right of Douglas Milne to be identified as the Author of this work has been asserted by him in accordance with the Copyright, Designs and Patents Act 1988

A catalogue record for this book is available from the British Library

Contains Ordnance Survey data © Crown copyright and database 2023 supported by out of copyright mapping 1945-1961

All rights reserved. No part of this publication may be reproduced, stored in a retrieval system, or transmitted in any form or by any means, electronic or mechanical, including photocopying and recording, unless expressly permitted by Pocket Mountains Ltd.

Printed by J Thomson Colour Printers, Glasgow

Introduction

South Argyll can truly be described as Scotland's hidden gem. Close enough to the Central Belt that parts of it are easily accessible by ferry, yet with a remoteness that gives the area a character all of its own, South Argyll is rich in history and prehistory. Several of Scotland's long-distance walking trails cross the area, including the Kintyre Way, the Loch Lomond and Cowal Way and the West Island Way. Parts of all of these are used in the walks in the chapters that follow.

History

The area that is now Argyll was known in Old Gaelic as *Airer Goidel*, meaning 'Coast of the Gaels'. This collection of 40 routes from throughout South Argyll explores an area which is nearly all coastal, whether on the peninsulas of Cowal or Kintyre, or on the Isles of Bute or Gigha.

Before it was Airer Goidel, the area that is now Argyll was Dal Riata, or Dalriada, a Gaelic kingdom which also included parts of the northeastern corner of Ireland. Its capital was at the hillfort of Dunadd, in Kilmartin Glen. The kingdom was formed through the arrival of the Scotti from Ulster in around 500AD. The Irish missionary Columba arrived in Kintyre in 563, hoping to spread Celtic Christianity among the pagan Picts, whose kingdom bordered on Dalriada.

In 843, the Dalriadan king Kenneth MacAlpin conquered the Picts, assimilating them into his kingdom and creating the Kingdom of Alba, now Scotland. But there was another enemy to defeat. In the late 8th century, Vikings had arrived in South Argyll from modern-day Norway. Though the first wave of Norsemen arrived as raiding parties, over time many chose to settle in Scotland and a hybrid Norse-Gaelic culture began to emerge. This culminated in the creation of the Lordship of the Isles under Somerled. Norse descendent Suibhe, Lord of Knapdale, built Castle Sween, while his son, Dugald, held Skipness Castle in 1261. Meanwhile the Stewarts built Rothesay Castle on Bute. Further castles were built at Tarbert and Dunaverty. The location of these castles emphasises that, in the days when boat was the fastest and safest method of travel, the sea was not a barrier but a highway.

Far later, the area around the Clyde estuary became known as the Glaswegian Riviera. As steamboats were introduced, towns such as Dunoon and Rothesay grew on the profits from Glasgow's working class heading 'doon the watter' in the summer, while middle-class villas sprung up at Tighnabruaich and at Kilchattan Bay on Bute.

The natural environment

The landscape is dominated by low heather-clad hills, gentle coastline and sandy beaches. Sea lochs stretch their way into Knapdale and around Cowal, while the great estuary of the Clyde surrounds the Isle of Bute and laps at the eastern shores of Kintyre before spilling out into the Atlantic.

The Gulf Stream, a current of warm seawater which flows from the Gulf of Mexico to Scotland's west coast, brings milder weather to South Argyll than more easterly parts of Scotland – indeed, palm trees can be found growing across the region. The mild Atlantic climate creates an unusual and diverse range of habitats for wildlife, attracting thousands of visiting wildfowl in winter. It is also a stronghold for rare and endangered native birds such as peregrine falcon.

Transport
There are regular bus services to the start of many of the walks in this guide, often with a connecting bus to Glasgow. Be aware that bus routes may have changed since the time of writing and so these should be checked before commencing your walk if you are relying upon it (travelinescotland.com). Although these routes might seem remote, many can be accessed from the Central Belt via ferry. Check timetables at calmac.co.uk.

Regular bus services run to all of the ferry ports. Ferries run between Colintraive in Cowal and Rhubodach on the Isle of Bute, between Portavadie in Cowal and Tarbert in Kintyre, and between Tayinloan in Kintyre and the Isle of Gigha.

Ferries to Dunoon and to the Isle of Bute can be accessed by train from Glasgow via the stations at Gourock and Wemyss Bay. The summer ferry service to Campbeltown can be accessed by train via the station at Ardrossan.

All of these ferries carry vehicles, and can save you the long but picturesque drive by Loch Lomond and Arrochar.

How to use this guide
This guide contains 40 coastal, low-level and hill walks. All are on obvious paths or tracks and are generally waymarked or are easy to follow. Nevertheless, before heading out for your walk, you should ask yourself three questions: Do you have the right gear? Do you know what the weather will be like? Do you have the knowledge and skills for the day?

You should not wholly rely on a smartphone to find your way. Using GPS can quickly drain your phone's battery, as can cold weather. A phone signal might not always be available. Always carry the relevant map and compass and learn how to use them. The relevant maps (OS Explorer 356, 357, 358, 362 and OL37) are listed within the text.

Accidents can happen anywhere. Always let someone know where you are going and when you expect to return. It's also a good idea to carry some spare provisions, a first aid kit, a whistle and a head torch in addition to your smartphone (with a back-up USB power pack) as a means of calling for help.

Always check the weather and dress appropriately. Wear good-quality walking boots, and carry warm, waterproof clothing, even if you don't think you'll need it. Walking poles are always handy.

In summer, *culicoides impunctatus*, also known as the West Coast midgie, can be a serious annoyance. Wearing light-coloured clothing with long sleeves and trouser legs and using an insect repellent and even a head net can help.

Ticks can be a more dangerous issue for walkers. In addition to the above measures, it can be worth tucking trousers into socks if walking in an area where ticks are prevalent and avoiding long grasses and undergrowth if possible. Check exposed skin at regular intervals and remove any ticks with a tick removal tool or tweezers.

On coastal routes, rocks can be slippery and waves can easily sweep you into the water. Check the tides before setting out.

Read through your route carefully, and be sure that it is within the capabilities of everyone in your group.

Access

The Land Reform (Scotland) Act of 2003 gives members of the public a right to access most Scottish land and inland waters for recreation, and landowners have a responsibility not to unreasonably prevent or deter access. However, key to the Act is that members of the public exercise their rights responsibly, as laid out in the Scottish Outdoor Access Code (outdooraccess-scotland.scot).

Take your litter home with you and pick up after your dog. Respect the environment and private property, and do not damage fences and crops. Close all gates behind you. Dogs should be kept under strict control, particularly in the spring and early summer when they could disturb ground-nesting birds. Do not enter a field with your dog if there are lambs, calves or other young farm animals. If you enter a field where there are animals, keep your dog on a short lead as far away from the animals as possible. If cattle become aggressive, keep calm, let your dog go, and take the shortest, safest route out of the field.

Large areas of Knapdale are home to coastal temperate rainforest – as ecologically important as tropical rainforest but much rarer. Variously known as Atlantic woodland, Celtic Rainforest or Scotland's Rainforest, it is made up of native tree species such as sessile oak, downy birch and European ash. The Gulf Stream, a current of warm seawater which flows from the Gulf of Mexico to Scotland's west coast, brings consistent levels of rainfall and relatively warm temperatures, providing just the right conditions for some of the world's rarest mosses, liverworts and lichens.

Loch nan Torran, Loch Fuar-Bheinne, Dubh Loch and Loch Clachaig are an important breeding habitat for black-throated divers, and are collectively designated as a Special Protection Area. Similarly, Loch Sween, which contains maerl beds, a colony of volcano worm, and is home to one of Scotland's most important populations of native oyster, is designated as a Nature Conservation Marine Protected Area.

In 2009, a five-year trial to introduce beavers into Knapdale was begun when 11 of the animals were released. Run jointly by the Scottish Wildlife Trust and the Royal Zoological Society of Scotland, and monitored by Scottish Natural Heritage, the trial was a success. The beavers were allowed to remain permanently, and were given protected status as a native species.

Knapdale

1. **Arichonan Township** — 8
   Visit the haunting remains of a Highland Clearance village

2. **Barnluasgan Oakwood** — 10
   Visit at dawn or dusk and you might catch a glimpse of the elusive Eurasian beaver

3. **The Loch Coille-Bharr Trail** — 12
   Look out for beavers in this easy saunter around a beautiful loch

4. **Taynish National Nature Reserve** — 14
   Explore the rare Celtic Rainforest in this ramble around the Taynish peninsula

5. **Ardrishaig circular** — 16
   Beginning at the eastern end of the Crinan Canal, climb the hill behind the village of Ardrishaig

6. **The Steallair Dubh** — 18
   Explore a cave once occupied by St Columba before tracing an ancient route across the slopes of Cruach nan Lochan

7. **Dùn a' Choin Duibh** — 20
   This woodland trail leads to an ancient Celtic hillfort

1 KNAPDALE

Arichonan Township

Distance 2.1km **Time** 45 minutes
Terrain hill tracks with some ascent
Map OS Explorer 358 **Access** no public transport to the start

Climb to the poignant ruins of the village of Arichonan in this short walk. A quiet and picturesque location today, with fine views along the narrow channel of Caol Scotnish and beyond into Loch Sween, it was the scene of a riot during the Highland Clearances.

Begin at the Forestry Commission's Glean a' Gealbhan car park, 4.5km west of Bellanoch along the B8025. Glean a' Gealbhan is part of Knapdale Forest, a relic of the Atlantic oakwoods which first took root some 10,000 years ago at the end of the last ice age.

In the 1800s, oak trees were coppiced and burnt to make charcoal, which was used to power the iron furnaces of the nascent Industrial Revolution. This practice gave Glean a' Gealbhan, or the Glen of Burning, its name.

Returning to the entrance to the car park, cross the road to follow an unsurfaced foot track up the hill. Ascend steadily before levelling out and swinging in a wide U-turn to walk westwards across the open hillside and then entering woodland. Look out for lichens and mosses, which thrive in the damp, clear air of this part of Knapdale.

The track soon becomes an enchanting old road through the trees, before emerging at the haunting remains of Arichonan Township.

Arichonan, from the Gaelic for 'Conan's Shieling', dates back to the 1600s. The land was feued in 1654 by the Campbells of Auchenbreck to Neil MacNeil from South Knapdale. It was bought by Neil Malcolm of Poltalloch at the beginning of the 19th century.

On Whitsunday 1848, Malcolm

ARICHONAN TOWNSHIP

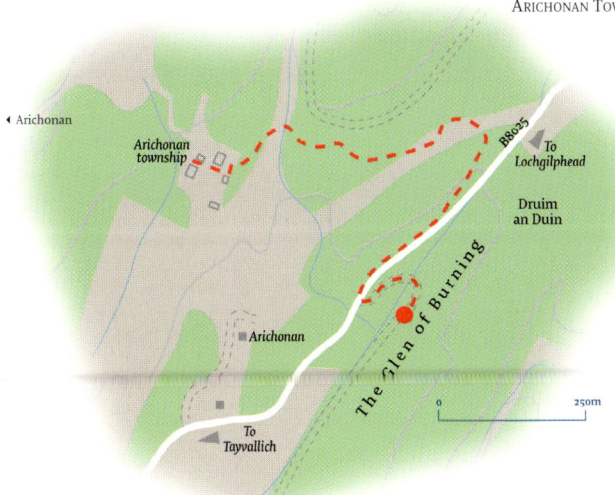

terminated his tenants' leases, with the intention of replacing them with sheep. He had bought land in Australia and wanted to move his tenants there. The villagers were told 'to flit and remove themselves and their wives, bairns, families, servants, subtenants, cottars, dependants, goods and gear'.

Unsurprisingly, the villagers did not want to lose their homes and livelihood, and instead of leaving quietly, they chose to stay and fight. They were soon joined by others from nearby townships.

The local police were called to enforce the evictions, prompting the villagers to arm themselves with sticks and stones and to riot. It became so violent that there were calls for the military to aid the police. William Martin, the estate factor, reported that he had been dragged 'half over a dyke'.

Four tenants were arrested. Catherine Campbell, Mary Adams, Neil McMillan and Duncan McLean were found guilty of resisting the eviction and imprisoned at Inverary Jail. Records of their imprisonment are still held at the jail.

Nevertheless, many people from Arichonan and the surrounding villages did emigrate to Canada and Australia in search of new beginnings. The McLeans of Arichonan were one of the families who went to Canada, settling in Ekfrid Township in Middlesex County.

The two more substantial ruins at the top end of the village are the remains of the shepherd's house, built after the evictions using stones salvaged from the walls of the villagers' houses.

When you have finished exploring the atmospheric remnants of Arichonan, return by the same route.

Barnluasgan Oakwood

Distance 2.8km **Time** 1 hour
Terrain gravel surfaced path throughout; several steep slopes **Map** OS Explorer 358
Access bus to war memorial at Tayvallich-Achnamara junction from Lochgilphead and Tayvallich

Climb to explore the ancient Atlantic oakwoods between Loch Barnluasgan and Loch Linne, before strolling around picturesque Loch Barnluasgan, keeping an eye out for the Eurasian beavers that live in the loch. These shy animals are most active at dawn and dusk.

This walk can be reduced to an easy half-hour saunter around the loch by missing out the climb up the hill.

Beavers are native to Scotland, but were hunted to extinction for their fur and castoreum, an oil used for scents and flavouring, in the 16th century. In 2009, a colony of beavers from Norway were introduced at Loch Barnluasgan, and were the subject of the Scottish Beaver Trial, which ran until 2014. In 2016, following a consultation, the Scottish government announced that the beavers were here to stay. In 2019, they became a legally-protected native species.

Beavers are natural engineers. Their ability to manipulate their environment to produce wetland habitats encourages native woodland and improves conditions for a wide range of species, including dragonflies, otters and fish. However, they must be carefully managed to minimise damage to agricultural land.

The walk begins at the Forestry Commission's Barnluasgan car park, 8om along the road to Achnamara from its junction with the B8025.

Go down the steps at the entrance to the car park, turning right to follow the path beneath a canopy of alder trees along

BARNLUASGAN OAKWOOD

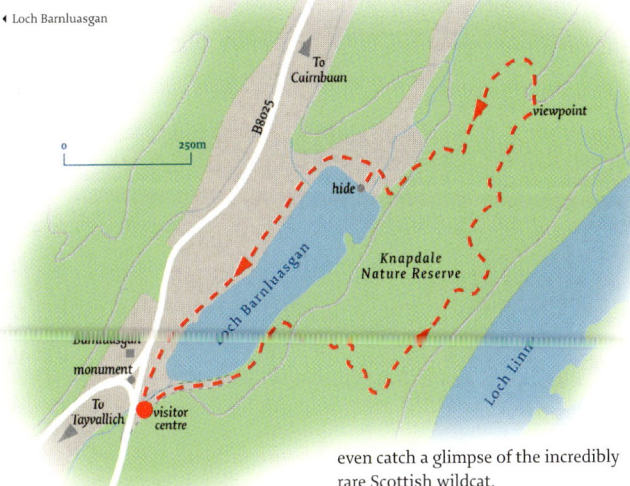

◀ Loch Barnluasgan

the southern shore of Loch Barnluasgan. Watch out for evidence of beaver activity such as stripped branches and felled trees as you skirt around the loch. Pass a small jetty, before turning right to ascend a flight of stone steps which winds steeply up the hill, offering good views back across the loch.

Soon, the climb eases, levelling out to pass through oak woodland along an undulating ridge, with occasional views of Loch Linne through the trees. This is an excellent example of Scotland's rainforest, and it is worth taking the time to examine the lichens, mosses and liverworts that make the area internationally important. Beavers are not the only animals at Barnluasgan. Red squirrel scamper around these trees. Roe deer and red deer live in the forest, and if you are lucky, you might even catch a glimpse of the incredibly rare Scottish wildcat.

Another flight of stone steps leads to a bench with views over Loch Barnluasgan and, in the distance, Loch Coille-Bharr. Drop down to meander through oak trees once more, before descending a very steep flight of stone steps to meet the lochside path again. Turn right to continue your circumnavigation of the loch.

Reaching a junction, a brief diversion along an unsurfaced track towards the water leads to a wildlife hide from which the entire loch can be seen.

The hide is an excellent place to look out for beavers. Watch out for the nose, eyes and ears just above the surface of the loch. Keep an eye open for bats, as well as birds such as buzzards, eagles and osprey.

Back on the main track, continue around the loch, following the path back to the car park.

The Loch Coille-Bharr Trail

Distance 5.2km **Time** 1 hour 30
Terrain surfaced and unsurfaced tracks, short section of road; some brief climbs
Map OS Explorer 358 **Access** buses to the war memorial at the Tayvallich-Achnamara junction from Lochgilphead and Tayvallich

Like nearby Loch Barnluasgan, Loch Coille-Bharr is home to a colony of beavers and, if you are lucky, you might catch a glimpse of them at dawn or dusk. Either way, you can't miss the signs of their activity in this beautiful circuit through ancient oakwoods.

The walk begins in the Forestry Commission's Loch Coille a'Bharra car park, 3km west along the B8025 from Bellanoch. It follows a red waymarked trail around the loch. Go around the gate by an information board and walk along the rough forestry road.

At a sign for Kilmory Oib, turn down the grassy track which leads to the remains of the settlement. The township is documented from the 17th century, but look out for an early Christian cross-marked stone, which dates from the 8th or 9th century. It is not known when or why Kilmory Oib was abandoned, but documentary evidence suggests that it was not long after a riot at nearby Arichonan, when villagers resisted eviction. Neil Malcolm of Poltalloch owned both of the townships, and wanted to turn the land over to sheep. Tenants from Kilmory took part in the Arichonan riot, fearful that they would suffer the same fate.

The path swings around the abandoned village before turning right onto the main track again. The ruins of Kilmory Mill are further along the track. The age of the building is unknown, although the 'meal mill of Coilebar' is mentioned as far back as 1490. Corn was ground using a

THE LOCH COILLE-BHARR TRAIL

◀ Evidence of beaver activity

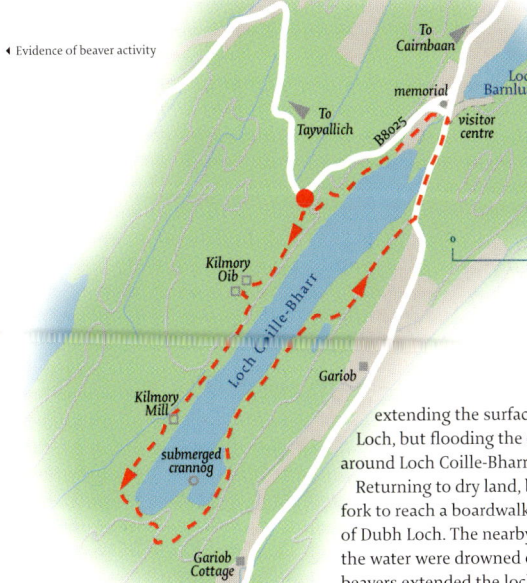

waterwheel, which was housed in the archway at the side of the building. It went out of use at the beginning of the 20th century.

Bear left to swing around the end of the loch, and climb steeply up and over a small hill. Turn left again at the next junction, descending to traverse an undulating woodland track on the southern shore. At a junction, drop left to walk along a floating pontoon. This pontoon was installed by Forestry and Land Scotland after a family of beavers dammed the outflows from Dubh Loch into Loch Coille-Bharr in 2009, greatly extending the surface area of Dubh Loch, but flooding the original path around Loch Coille-Bharr.

Returning to dry land, bear right at a fork to reach a boardwalk with fine views of Dubh Loch. The nearby dead trees in the water were drowned out when the beavers extended the loch. Beavers don't like feeding very far from water. They build dams to extend their feeding area, or to prevent the entrance to their lodge from being exposed. The family has since moved away and the water is slowly receding, creating a wetland that has resulted in a huge boost to biodiversity.

Beyond the platform, the path becomes a vehicle track which rises to join a country road. Continue along the road by the lochside. Approaching a war memorial, turn left through a gate to take a path across a field. The path enters woodland beyond another gate, following the loch shore for a little before winding through trees to return to the car park.

Taynish National Nature Reserve

Distance 7.5km **Time** 2 hours 15 **Terrain** surfaced and unsurfaced tracks; mild ascents **Map** OS Explorer 358 **Access** no public transport to the start; the nearest bus service from Lochgilphead is to Tayvallich, 2km from the start

The Atlantic oak woodland at Taynish is a temperate rainforest which has survived for more than 7000 years. On this walk you might see some of the wealth of wildlife that lives in this tranquil corner of Scotland.

The route begins at the reserve's car park, 2km south of Tayvallich. Walk past the sign forbidding unauthorised vehicles, and follow the road through the trees. In 1650, MacNeill, the Laird of the Ross Estate, built Taynish House at the far end of the peninsula. This estate road was built by Campbell of Inverneill around 1800. A cottage on the right was the former gatehouse.

After around 2km, turn right through a gate. The field beside the gate is known as Katie Campbell's Field. Katie was an 18th-century farm girl who lost her foot in a reaping accident. It is said that the foot was pickled and eventually buried with her.

The path parallels the road for a little while before going through a second gate and turning downhill towards a picnic area at the Linne Mhuirich. Look out for eider ducks, which feed on saltwater molluscs. White-tailed sea eagles can sometimes be spotted soaring above. Common sandpipers, curlew, herons and oystercatchers probe the saltmarsh.

Return to the second gate, turning right to continue along the path. Just before another gate, turn towards the Piggery (signposted). Built around 1800, the Piggery provided five-star accommodation for the pigs of Taynish Farm.

Return to the gate and go through it to

TAYNISH NATIONAL NATURE RESERVE

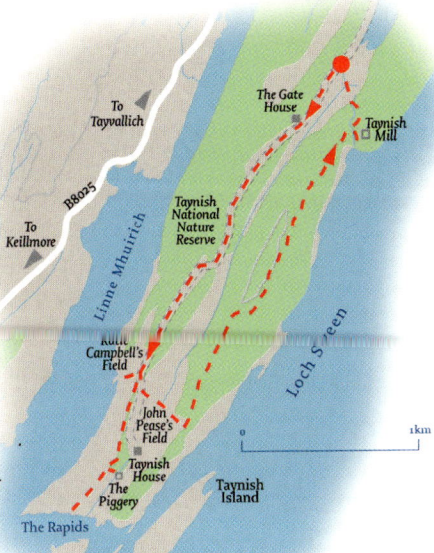

◀ Taynish Mill

head for the shore, where water rushing through the narrow channel between Loch Sween and the Linne Mhuirich creates rapids. In the summer, ospreys can often be seen fishing here. The building on the left is an otter hide. Otters fish for crabs and fish, returning to the shore to devour their catch on a favourite rock.

Retrace your steps to the gate by Katie Campbell's Field and turn right to continue along the road. After a gate, turn immediately left to traverse a surfaced path across John Pease's Field. Pease was the son of the last owner of Taynish Estate and the field is dotted with the beeches, sycamores and limes that he loved.

Exit through a gate to enter the woodland beyond. This is part of the old road that followed the ridge from Taynish House to Duntaynish. The surfaced path soon becomes a gently undulating track through the lichen- and moss-covered oak trees. Holly, birch and other smaller trees nestle among the oaks and, in spring, the forest floor is carpeted with wildflowers. Loch Sween can be glimpsed through the trees. A better view may be gained at a convenient bench further down the track.

After several sets of stone steps, head downhill to a waterfall by the ruins of Taynish Mill. Built around 1724, the mill continued working for about 150 years.

Continue straight ahead to reach the shore of Loch Sween, where there is a stone seat engraved with a poem by William Blake.

Returning to the mill, take the path to the right of the ruin and follow it back to the car park.

Ardrishaig circular

Distance 6km **Time** 2 hours
Terrain good hill tracks and vehicle tracks; very damp underfoot in places
Map OS Explorer 358 **Access** bus to Ardrishaig from Lochgilphead, Campbeltown and Glasgow

Cruach Breacain, the hill above Ardrishaig, offers wonderful views across Loch Gilp and Loch Fyne to the Cowal Peninsula. The name of the village comes from the Gaelic *Aird Driseig*, meaning 'Height of the Small Bramble'. This scenic circuit scales the Cruach nam Bonnach face of Cruach Breacain. The final section of the route can be very muddy and boots are recommended.

The village sits at the eastern end of the Crinan Canal. Often called 'the most beautiful shortcut in the world', the 14km-long Crinan Canal connects Ardrishaig on Loch Gilp, a small inlet on Loch Fyne, with the Sound of Jura, providing a route between the Clyde and the Inner Hebrides without having to navigate the treacherous waters around the Mull of Kintyre. It was designed by engineer John Rennie and takes its name from the village of Crinan, at its western end. Work began in 1794 and although it opened in 1801 it was not completed until 1809.

The walk begins at the harbour at Ardrishaig. Construction on the harbour began in 1800, with later improvements made by Thomas Telford. The harbour consists of a 240m-long breakwater with a lighthouse at the far end. A pier was added in 1873 to accommodate passenger steamers from Glasgow. Today, the pier is used to ship timber, with around 30,000 tonnes passing through the harbour each year. This reduces the carbon footprint of road transport. A programme of refurbishment and modernisation has boosted capacity to 150,000 tonnes.

Starting just south of the canal basin,

ARDRISHAIG CIRCULAR

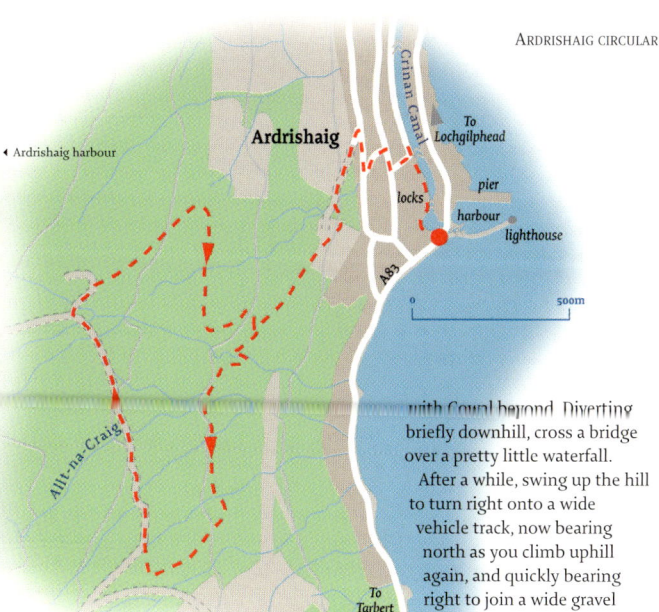

swing around the left of the basin and continue along the towpath. In 1847, four horses, two of them ridden by postilions in royal livery, trotted along this towpath, pulling a boat carrying Queen Victoria along the canal.

Meeting a road, take a sharp left to walk up the hill. Turn right at the top, then the first left to climb Glenfyne Crescent. Go right at the top. Turn uphill again onto a single-track road, following a sign for Inverneill and Tarbert. Bear left at a junction, following the cycle route to Inverneill, to stride along a surfaced path with excellent views across Loch Gilp, with Cowal beyond. Diverting briefly downhill, cross a bridge over a pretty little waterfall.

After a while, swing up the hill to turn right onto a wide vehicle track, now bearing north as you climb uphill again, and quickly bearing right to join a wide gravel surfaced road – one of the many forestry access roads which transect the hillside.

It is worth pausing for the view down Loch Fyne and across to Cowal.

Head along the road, climbing gently and turning right at a junction. Quickly arriving at a fork, bear right to amble down an overgrown road at the edge of some woodland. Swinging around and levelling out, the road soon becomes covered in a layer of earth.

Reaching the end of the road, turn left down a narrow but well-defined very muddy foot track. Squelch through the trees and bushes to join the outward route at a gateway, and follow it back to the beginning of the walk.

17

The Steallair Dubh

Distance 9.3km Time 2 hours 45
Terrain surfaced roads; hill tracks; very
damp underfoot Map OS Explorer 358
Access no public transport to the start

The Steallair Dubh, which means 'Black Cataract', is an ancient track which sticks to the high ground to the north of Loch Caolisport. It joined the villages of Achahoish and Kilmory, at the mouth of Loch Sween. Until the road along the northwestern shore of Loch Caolisport was built in around 1895, it was the main route between the two communities.

The route is shown on William Roy's Military Survey, completed in the aftermath of the Battle of Culloden.

This walk begins beside St Columba's Cave, 4.75km along the road to Ellary from its junction with the B8024 at Achahoish. There is limited parking at the cave, but further parking is available 160m back down the road towards Achahoish (marked 'No Overnight Parking').

The cave is impressive and worth a look before you begin your walk. It is said to have been occupied by Columba in 563 as he travelled to meet Conall mac Comgaill, king of Dalriada, to gain permission to set up a monastery on Iona. The cave contains a stone altar and a basin carved into the rock which would have held holy water. A cross is carved into the wall above the altar. Excavations in the 20th century confirmed that the cave was in use as far back as the stone age. A 13th-century chapel sits near the cave mouth.

Follow the road back along the edge of Loch Caolisport towards Achahoish, passing some holiday cottages. The road, which is virtually traffic free, is very peaceful and is a splendid lochside stroll.

THE STEALLAIR DUBH

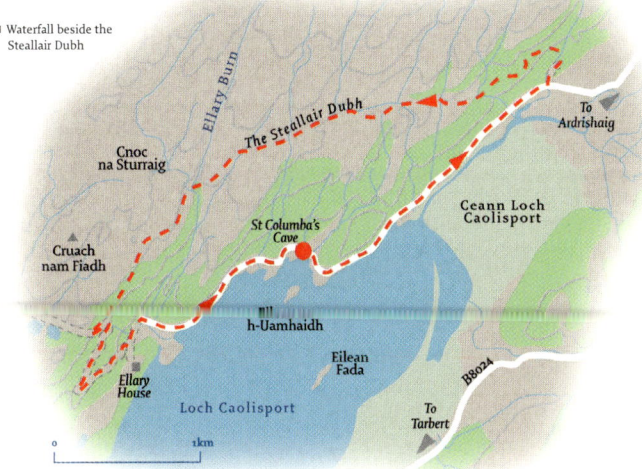

◀ Waterfall beside the Steallair Dubh

After 2.2km, where the road veers to the right, turn left to follow a muddy vehicle track up the hill through woodland.

Keep straight ahead at a junction, briefly leaving the trees to cross open hillside beneath the slopes of Cruach nan Lochan. Go through a metal gate to continue over a wide grassy plain where the route is easily discernible, although the grass can get very long.

Crossing a burn by a wooden bridge and rounding a corner you are suddenly faced with a striking waterfall.

The path undulates across the hillside, following the line of some telegraph poles for a little before rounding a small hillock and dropping gently into a gorge. As you make your way through the gorge, the view ahead, across the mouth of Loch Caolisport with the top end of the Isle of Gigha in the distance, begins to open out, becoming increasingly magnificent as you begin to climb again.

Pass another waterfall and climb to reach a bench at a junction with a more formal surfaced vehicle track. The Steallair Dubh continues along the vehicle track, eventually arriving at Loch Sween, but instead, take a hard left to drop steeply down the hill in a couple of wide switchbacks, passing rhododendrons and open woodland.

Stay on the main road as you pass Ellary House. Reaching a gate, go through it, turning left at the junction immediately beyond to continue down the hill. The road drops down to the shore to quickly return to St Columba's Cave.

Dùn a' Choin Duibh

Distance 2.7km **Time** 1 hour
Terrain mostly surfaced track, unsurfaced woodland track up to the fort; some steep ascents **Map** OS Explorer 357
Access bus to Torinturk from Tarbert and Kilberry

This short circular walk climbs through Torinturk Forest, passing a Bronze Age cairn to reach the remains of an ancient hillfort, Dùn a' Choin Duibh. Legend tells of the great hunter Torquil Mor, who lived in the Dun and died fighting a wild boar. Indeed, Torinturk translates as 'the hill of the boar'. The fort offers magnificent views across West Loch Tarbert to Kintyre, and beyond to Arran.

A peaceful woodland walk throughout, the forest is an ideal habitat for voles, a favourite snack for the buzzards and owls that hunt among the trees. Look out for anthills, constructed by wood ants from the needles of spruce and other conifers that carpet the forest floor.

The route follows blue waymarkers all the way and begins in the Forestry Commission's Torinturk car park, accessed via a rough single-track road which leads up the hill from the village of Torinturk. From the car park, continue along the road signposted for the Torinturk walk. In late spring, the forest is awash with bluebells. The road, which is straight and wide, climbs gently through the trees.

Swinging around a rocky outcrop, the road comes to an end at a small turning circle. Turn right on a raised gravel track which leads steeply up the hill through the forest, levelling out after a while to arrive at the very wide, open clearing of the Achaglachgach Cairns.

There are two distinct cairns here. The smaller, a Bronze Age cairn named Diarmid's Grave, or the Giant's Grave, is

DÙN A' CHOIN DUIBH

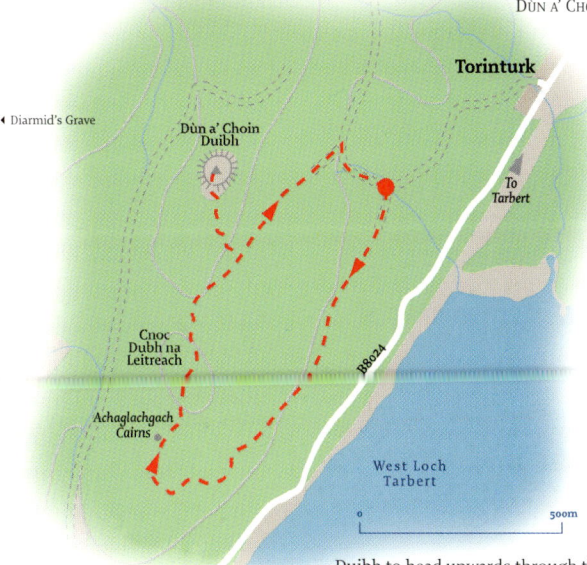

marked by a triangular upright stone and dates from between 2500 and 600BC. Diarmid O'Dhuine was a mythical hero under the command of Finn MacCool. The story of Diarmid and Grainne, Finn's girlfriend, is one of the great sagas of both medieval Scotland and Ireland. Diarmid is said to be the founder of Clan Campbell. The larger cairn, erected by Neolithic farming communities, is thought to date from between 4000 and 2000BC.

Another raised moss-covered track leads off to the right of the cairns. It climbs very steeply to a thoughtfully placed bench at the top of the hill.

After a while, turn left into the forest, crossing a little wooden bridge and following a signpost for Dùn a' Choin Duibh to head upwards through the trees. The track isn't obvious, but keep an eye open for the blue waymark posts that signal the route.

A heather-clad hilltop is crowned with the atmospheric remains of Dùn a' Choin Duibh. The fort dates from around the 6th century and was occupied for 500 years. Along the wall to the left, a small doorway led to a chamber, now collapsed which, according to legend, housed a black wolfhound guarding the fort and gave it its name, which translates as 'the Fort of the Black Dog'.

Having explored the fort, retrace your steps through the trees to return to the main path, turning left to stride down the hill to a junction. Bear right here to head back down to the car park.

Antony Gormley's GRIP looking out towards Ailsa Craig from Saddell Bay ▶

The long, narrow finger of land that makes up Kintyre stretches down from the rest of Scotland until it almost touches the coast of Antrim in Northern Ireland. Around 64km long and only 13km wide at its widest point, it is separated from Knapdale by West Loch Tarbert, which almost, but not quite, turns Kintyre into an island.

In 1098, Magnus Barelegs, a Norse king who had gained his nickname by his adoption of the knee-length tunic favoured in the Scottish islands, formed a treaty with the King of Scots in which the Norse could lay claim to all the islands off the west coast which were separated by water navigable by a boat with the rudder set. But Magnus had his eye on Kintyre – it was, he said, 'more valuable than the best of all the Hebridean islands' – and cheated the King of Scots by having his men drag him in a local fishing skiff across the isthmus. Norsemen subsequently settled in Kintyre, and their farm and landscape names survive into the present day: Carradale, Saddell, Skipness, Muasdale and Ormsary, and many other examples, were named by the Norse incomers.

At the height of The Beatles' success, Paul McCartney bought a farm in Kintyre. The area inspired some of his most famous songs, including *The Long and Winding Road* (the A83 down Kintyre's west coast) and, of course, *Mull of Kintyre*.

Kintyre

1. **The White Shore at Port Ban** 24
   Take this short walk along East Loch Tarbert to a secluded beach

2. **The Corranbuie Trail** 26
   Climb high above Tarbert to enjoy fine views across Loch Fyne

3. **Dùn Skeig** 28
   Discover an ancient hillfort before returning by the coast

4. **Skipness Castle** 30
   Explore the grounds of Skipness Castle and its medieval chapel

5. **Deer Hill** 32
   This hill boasts stunning views over the Kilbrannan Sound

6. **Carradale Canter** 34
   Visit Carradale's superb beach and discover an ancient island fort

7. **Saddell Bay** 36
   View an historic castle and a haunting modern sculpture on this coastal trail

8. **Machrihanish and the Gauldrons** 38
   Wildlife abounds in this easy ramble on a dramatic stretch of coast

9. **Beinn Ghuilean** 40
   Climb from the harbour to a hill high above Campbeltown

10. **Davaar Island and the Crucifixion Cave** 42
    Cross the causeway to discover an historic lighthouse and unusual work of art

11. **Glenramskill Old Road** 44
    From the east of Campbeltown, cross a headland, then return via the coast

12. **The Mull of Kintyre** 46
    A long and winding (and very steep) road leads down to a lighthouse perched high on a cliff

13. **Keil Caves and Dunaverty Rock** 48
    Follow in the footsteps of a Celtic saint before visiting the site of a 17th-century castle

KINTYRE

The White Shore at Port Ban

Distance 3km **Time** 1 hour
Terrain surfaced roads, unsurfaced forest tracks **Map** OS Explorer 357 **Access** bus to Tarbert from Lochgilphead, Campbeltown and Glasgow

This short walk leads from the picturesque conservation village of Tarbert along the northern side of Tarbert Harbour and East Loch Tarbert to arrive at a small and secluded shell and pebble beach known as the White Shore.

Tarbert Harbour is the focal point of the village, and is always busy. You can watch the catch being landed, or admire the yachts, cruisers and traditional boats that line the pontoons of the marina.

The harbour was designed by Thomas Telford, as part of a huge programme of canal, road and bridge construction between 1806 and 1821 by the Commissioners for Highland Roads and Bridges, with the aim of alleviating social problems in the Highlands by improving communication. A square quay, an artificial island known as the Beilding, sits in the middle of the harbour. It was used to help haul sailing vessels into the harbour in stormy weather.

The walk begins at the harbour, at the junction of Harbour Street and Barmore Road. Walk around the harbour, keeping the water on your right. Look out for the replica of a Loch Fyne Skiff moored a few metres out into the bay.

These timber boats, propelled by oar and sail, were a 19th-century design particular to the Loch Fyne area. They came in various sizes up to 10.5m and had a steeply sloping mast at the front of the boat, leaving plenty of working space in the centre. Built around Tarbert and known as a Loch Fyne Skiff, the boats had a crew of five and were used mainly in the herring fishing industry which developed on Loch Fyne during the 18th

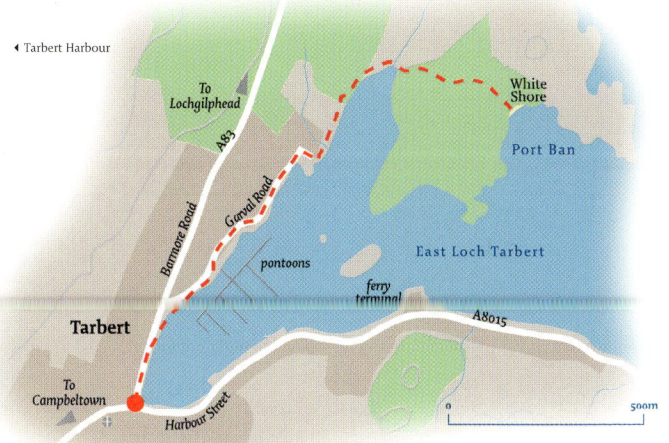

◀ Tarbert Harbour

and early 19th centuries. Sadly, boat building is no longer a viable industry, but this replica skiff, the *Wee Dooker*, was built in Tarbert in 2009 using traditional boat-building skills.

Beyond the skiff, take the lower path to walk along the harbourside. Approaching a car park, bear left uphill to continue along Garval Road. At a crossroads, turn back down towards the sea before heading left along a very narrow gravel path beyond the last house, signposted as the White Shore Walk.

Almost immediately enter woodland, zigzagging briefly uphill before continuing up steps. Carry straight on ahead at a junction, dropping to cross a bridge over a burn and staying relatively close to the shore before heading inland (eastwards) through the woods. Turn left at a junction, ascending gently to cross a boardwalk across a bog.

Soon the track leaves the trees to descend to a small bay, the White Shore, which looks out across the mouth of East Loch Tarbert. The bay is also known as Port Ban from the Gaelic, meaning 'the White Harbour'.

Look closely at the white sand and you will see that it is actually made up of crushed shells. Many winkles, anemones and mussels can be found clinging to the rocks at low tide when the remains of a jetty are also revealed on the left. This was in use before Tarbert Harbour was constructed in the early 19th century.

Having enjoyed the beach, retrace your steps back to Tarbert.

The Corranbuie Trail

Distance 5.3km **Time** 1 hour 45
Terrain well-defined hill tracks; steep ascents **Map** OS Explorer 357
Access bus to Tarbert from Lochgilphead, Campbeltown and Glasgow

Climb past Tarbert Castle onto the lower slopes beneath Cruach an t-Sorchain, the peak which rises south of Tarbert. There are several viewpoints off the track, each offering stunning views over Tarbert and Loch Fyne. Roe and sika deer can sometimes be spotted amongst the trees as you climb, while golden eagles soar overhead. The route follows blue waymarkers throughout.

Tarbert became a Royal Burgh during the reign of Robert the Bruce. It expanded rapidly in the early 19th century, when its fishing fleet grew as a result of adopting ring-net fishing for herring.

Beginning at Tarbert Harbour, walk along the quay, keeping the water on your left. Turn right to climb steps signposted for Tarbert Castle. Go through a kissing gate to pass the entrance to the castle. What is now Tarbert Castle was probably a simple hillfort until 1292, when it became a royal castle under John Balliol. His successor, Robert the Bruce, realising the strategic importance of the isthmus between East and West Lochs Tarbert, set about extending it in 1325, adding a courtyard, towers, a hall, and a chapel, as well as places for artisans to work.

The tower, which is all that remains of the castle today, was probably added by James IV in 1494. That same year, he summoned his parliament to meet at Tarbert to discuss means of pacifying the turbulent areas of Kintyre and the Islands.

THE CORRANBUIE TRAIL

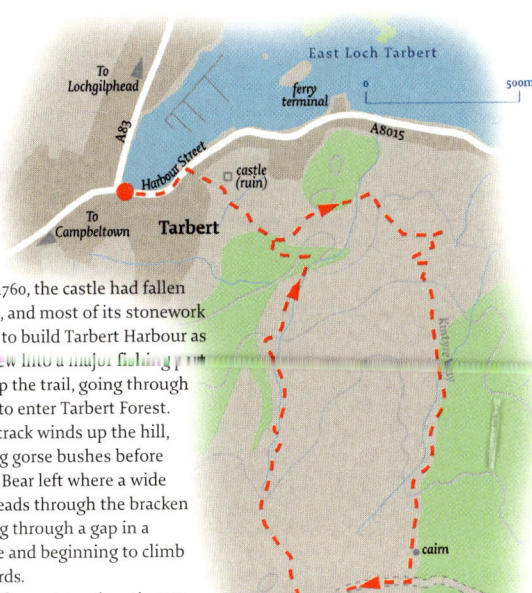

However, by 1760, the castle had fallen into disrepair, and most of its stonework was removed to build Tarbert Harbour as the village grew into a major fishing port.

Continue up the trail, going through another gate to enter Tarbert Forest. The obvious track winds up the hill, circumventing gorse bushes before levelling out. Bear left where a wide grassy track leads through the bracken before passing through a gap in a drystane dyke and beginning to climb steeply upwards.

Bear left at the next two junctions to reach a viewpoint, giving an impressive panorama across Loch Fyne towards the Cowal Peninsula. Portavadie can be seen on the distant shore, with the ferry zipping backwards and forwards. Looking north, beyond Port Ban and Barmore Island, the Knapdale coast stretches all the way to Lochgilphead.

Return to the main path and continue up the relentlessly steep hill. Rounding a corner, you come to the Tarbert Millennium Cairn, erected in 2000 by a local man to celebrate the birth of his nephews. The path to the left leads to a picnic bench with excellent views across the hills.

Climb on past the cairn, turning right onto a vehicle track and following it across the hillside. Turn right at a waypoint after 300m, striking off down the hill on another track. After 1km, look out for a damp path on the left, leading across heather-covered slopes to a fine view across Tarbert Bay, with the castle in the foreground and Loch Fyne stretching out behind it. Back on the main path, continue down the hill to join the outward trail and follow it back to the start of the walk.

◀ Tarbert Castle

Dùn Skeig

Distance 6.4km **Time** 2 hours
Terrain surfaced and unsurfaced tracks, some steep; one waterlogged section
Map OS Explorer 357 **Access** bus to Clachan from Lochgilphead, Glasgow and Campbeltown

Dùn Skeig, meaning 'Hawthorn Fort', is a prominent hill which stands sentinel over the entrance to West Loch Tarbert. It is crowned by the vitrified remains of an Iron Age fort and offers superb views across the loch and over the Sound of Jura. This walk climbs to the summit before dropping down to the shore to encircle the hill.

It begins by the gate of Kilcalmonell Parish Church in Clachan, one of the oldest villages in the area. The church, built in around 1760 to replace an earlier building, is worth exploring for the early Christian and medieval carved stones in its graveyard.

Stroll along the gravel drive which leads from the gate. Turn left onto the main road, crossing the Clachan Burn and climbing steeply out of the village.

After 500m, leave the road beside a large wooden shed, turning left to walk up an unsurfaced vehicle track. This is the Ferry Road, an old route from Clachan to the jetty at Portachoillan.

Go through a gate, climbing gently uphill between two drystane dykes. Dun Skeig can be seen to the left, with its trig point prominent on the horizon.

As the track begins to descend, offering grand views across West Loch Tarbert to the shores of Knapdale, turn through a rusty old gate on the left to stride over rough and occasionally boggy pasture towards the summit of Dùn Skeig.

DÙN SKEIG

Perched at the top of the hill is the Iron Age complex which gave Dùn Skeig its name. There have been three successive *duns* on the site, with each being cannibalised to build its successor. The stunning views across the Sound of Jura to Islay, Jura and, closer to shore, Gigha, and its commanding position overlooking the entrance to a strategically crucial waterway make clear the reason why the site was selected as a defensive position. Ensconced at the top of the steep-sided hilltop and surrounded by thick defensive walls, the chief of the fort would have felt secure from attack and king of all that he could see.

Return to the gate and continue down the hill. The path here is lined with trees, and is covered in bluebells in the spring. Beyond another gate, follow a marked route around the grounds of a house, joining a vehicle track to descend to a crossroads at the hamlet of Portachoillan. From the mid-19th century, passengers were rowed across West Loch Tarbert from here to Ardpatrick on the far shore. The service stopped in the 1930s, but the jetty can still be seen.

Turn left to set off along an old road along the shore beneath the steep western slopes of Dùn Skeig. Keep an eye out for otters as you pass a sandy bay. Beyond the bay, the road can become waterlogged, but persevere to go through another gate by some sheep pens.

Further on, swing inland beside the Clachan Burn, bearing right to leave the road through an old stone gateway. Walk along an unsurfaced track, through another gate and across a pasture, still parallel to the Clachan Burn. Go through an ornate cast-iron gate, turning right to return to Clachan.

◀ Dùn Skeig overlooking the Sound of Jura

Skipness Castle

Distance 4.2km **Time** 1 hour 15
Terrain mostly good paths; the return route through the dell can be muddy but may be omitted **Map** OS Explorer 357
Access bus to Skipness from Tarbert and Lochgilphead

The impressive 13th-century Skipness Castle sits just outside the village of Skipness. This short but beautiful walk visits the castle, its chapel and an attractive sandy bay, before returning through an idyllic wooded dell.

The walk begins in the castle's visitors' car park. To get there take the B8001, which leaves the A83 southwest of Tarbert, then follow the tourist signs for Skipness Castle. The drive along the rocky shore towards Skipness is breathtaking. Look out for a Second World War observation post from Skipness Bombing Range above the entrance to the village. Cross an old stone bridge, and the car park is immediately on the left.

From the car park, cross the road to pass between two cast-iron pillars. An ornate circular lodge, topped with a parapet, sits just inside the gate. This is the driveway of Skipness Estate. Head along the drive, passing through woodland. Bear right to cross a bridge over the Eas Fhaolain and turn left at the junction beyond. Skipness Castle can be seen ahead. It is worth a short diversion to explore the castle.

The castle guards the northern entrance to Kilbrannan Sound, the stretch of water between Kintyre and Arran. It dates from at least 1261, when it belonged to the MacSweens. As Tarbert Castle, 12km further north, grew in importance, Skipness became a domesticated towerhouse. It was converted into farm

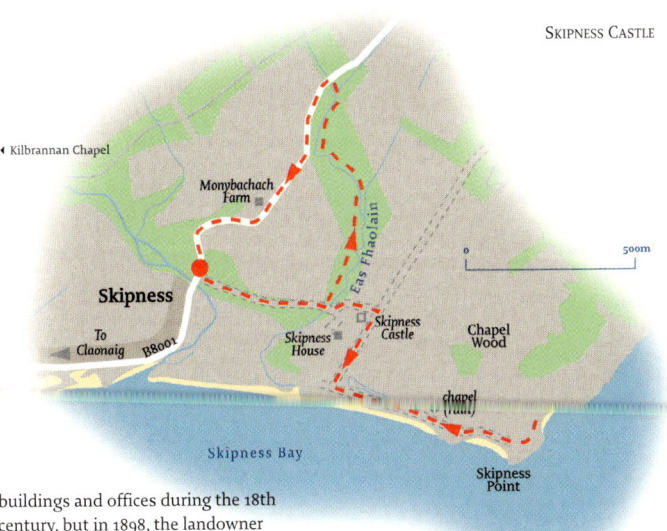

buildings and offices during the 18th century, but in 1898, the landowner R C Graham began restoration work.

Return to the road and continue beyond the castle to a cottage. Turn downhill towards the sea and follow the track through a gate and along the edge of a field. At the corner, by another gate, turn left to parallel the shore and reach the ruins of Kilbrannan Chapel.

The chapel, dedicated to St Brendan, is considered to date from the late 13th or early 14th century. It is thought to have been constructed by the same masons who worked on extensions to the castle. The graveyard is notable for its medieval tombstones, now housed in protective boxes. Just beyond the chapel, a huge arrow is set into the ground. It indicated the correct approach to Skipness Bombing Range, a Second World War offshore range which was used for both bombing and torpedo practice.

Continue along the track, going through a gate to pass a sandy bay and reach Skipness Point, where there are great views across to the Isle of Arran. Look out for birds such as oystercatchers, shags and gulls.

Retrace your steps back to cross the bridge over the Eas Fhaolain again, turning immediately right along a muddy track which leads off along the edge of the burn through a wooded dell. In spring the woodland floor is carpeted with snowdrops and, in summer, wild garlic.

Skip over a stone bridge across the burn, and continue upstream on the other side. Emerging from the trees onto a narrow road, turn left. Wander down the road through Monybachach Farm and back to the car park.

Deer Hill

Distance 5.8km **Time** 2 hours
Terrain good surfaced and unsurfaced tracks; some steep inclines and descents
Map OS Explorer 356 **Access** bus to Carradale from Campbeltown

Cnoc nan Gabhar translates from Gaelic as the 'Rock of the Goat', but this lovely little peak is known locally as Deer Hill.

There are indeed deer on the hill – look out for red and roe deer amongst the mature trees, and fallow and sika deer in the open glades around the younger trees. This route follows the Deer Hill Trail, which is identified by red waymarkers.

The walk begins in the Forestry Commission's Port Na Storm car park, along an unnamed minor road across the B879 from Carradale Primary School.

Leave the car park and turn left to follow a wide unsurfaced road up the hill. Reaching a junction, take a right turn to continue climbing along the edge of woodland, following a section of the Kintyre Way.

The waymarker at the next left is difficult to spot, but turn uphill here, where a rough vehicle track quickly narrows to a foot track which climbs steadily upwards, with occasional glimpses across the Kilbrannan Sound to Arran through the trees. Ailsa Craig is prominent to the southeast.

Reaching a junction by a signpost, turn left to leave the Kintyre Way behind. Curve steeply up the hill, swapping the trees for open moorland which is dotted with bright rhododendrons.

Look out here for moorland birds such as red and black grouse among the heather. Golden eagles, hen harriers, buzzards and kestrels may be seen circling overhead, searching for prey such as voles which live in the grassy areas around the

◀ Summit of Cnoc nan Gabhar

younger trees further down the hill.

Turn right by a Forestry Commission marker post, signposted for Cnoc nan Gabhar, to climb the rather muddy but short track to the summit, which is marked by a painted trig point.

The view is excellent from here. Cnoc nan Gabhar is on a peninsula which juts out into the Kilbrannan Sound, allowing almost all of Kintyre's east coast to be seen, as well as the whole length of Arran, where big hills such as Cir Mhòr, Beinn Bharrain and Beinn Tarsuinn are prominent. Ben Cruachan, the highest point in Argyll, is on the northern horizon, while Ailsa Craig and the Ayrshire coast sit to the southeast. Carradale, with its busy little harbour, is immediately below.

Return to the Forestry Commission marker post, turning right to continue south along the main path. After descending gently for a little, the path suddenly veers to the right, climbing steeply upwards before levelling out and heading south again. Reaching a craggy rockface, follow the path downhill. The descent is gentle at first, but quickly becomes very steep. The track soon enters woodland again and continues to drop down through the trees.

Reaching a junction with a forest vehicle track, turn left to join the Kintyre Way again, and carry on downhill. Walk along the vehicle track for 1.4km before turning right to return to the car park.

Carradale Canter

Distance 8.2km **Time** 2 hours 30
Terrain surfaced and unsurfaced roads and tracks **Map** OS Explorer 356
Access bus to Carradale from Campbeltown; be aware of tide times when accessing the fort

This delightful circuit explores the harbour at Carradale, turning inland only to return to the sea again to find an Iron Age hillfort.

The walk begins at the chocolate-box Carradale Harbour, with its colourful fishing boats. Follow the single-track road around the seafront from the harbour, keeping the sea on the right, turning left after 500m to follow a sign for the Broomfield Forest Walks through a gate. Head up the gravel track, bearing left at the top to cross a stile and follow an unsurfaced path across a grassy pasture.

Turn right onto a vehicle track, bearing right again at a junction, following the sign for Broomfield. The track quickly narrows, dropping down a hill to turn left onto a single-track road.

Follow the road down to a crossroads and turn right to walk along the B879, passing Carradale Village Hall. The cast-iron water wheel on the side of the building confirms that it was once a mill, used by the Paterson family for threshing oats.

Bear left through a gate after some farm buildings 200m beyond the hall. Turn right at a crosspaths, then left towards Carradale Bay (signposted) at the next junction, to stroll down a tree-lined caravan park access road beside Carradale Water.

Nearing the sea, bear right to go around a gate and wander down a gorse-lined

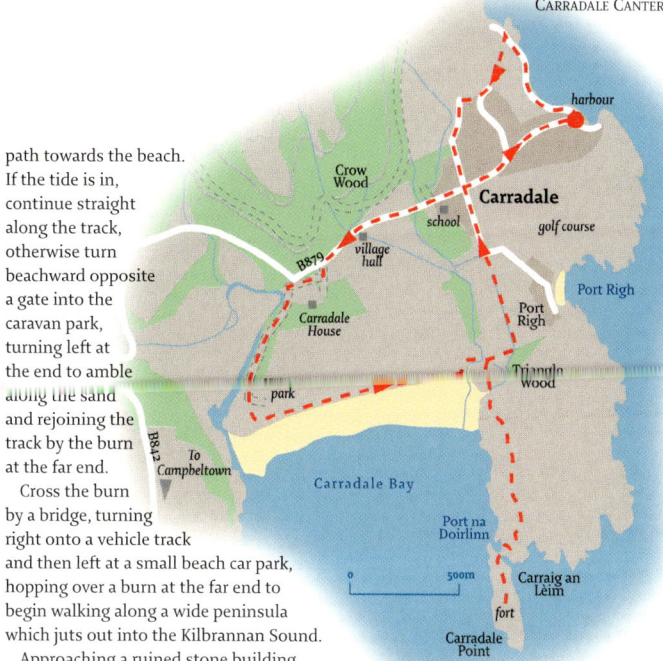

path towards the beach. If the tide is in, continue straight along the track, otherwise turn beachward opposite a gate into the caravan park, turning left at the end to amble along the sand and rejoining the track by the burn at the far end.

Cross the burn by a bridge, turning right onto a vehicle track and then left at a small beach car park, hopping over a burn at the far end to begin walking along a wide peninsula which juts out into the Kilbrannan Sound.

Approaching a ruined stone building, keep left to go through a gate. The path, which climbs through bracken and rhododendron, is overgrown but obvious. The bushes are sparser on the hilltop, where a pleasant track leads to the end of the peninsula. Keep an eye out for the herd of wild goats that live here. Watch the sea too, where you might spot basking sharks or leaping salmon.

Reaching the end, the track drops to a short tidal causeway, which is covered at high tide. Cross the causeway, keeping left at the far end to climb to the remains of a well-preserved vitrified fort. The oval-shaped fort walls were built of stone in a huge wooden framework. The heat that burned the fort to the ground more than 2000 years ago was so intense that the stonework melted and fused together.

Return along the peninsula to the car park, leaving by the vehicle track you used earlier, and following it as it veers left around a field. Continue through a gate, keeping straight on the road beyond.

Turn right at the crossroads, following the road through the village back to the harbour.

◀ Carradale Point looking back towards Carradale Bay

Saddell Bay

Distance 4km **Time** 1 hour 15
Terrain good surfaced and unsurfaced roads and tracks **Map** OS Explorer 356
Access bus to Saddell from Campbeltown and Carradale

The quiet glen where the Saddell Water flows into the Kilbrannan Sound was called 'Saddell', Norse for 'Sandy Valley', by Viking settlers more than 1000 years ago. There is plenty to see on this short, easy stroll, from historic carved stones to the location of a famous '70s pop video.

The walk begins in the small car park on the road up to Saddell Abbey, off the B842 in the centre of Saddell. Continue up the road to the abbey, entering the grounds by the gate.

The Vikings were defeated in the 12th century by the great Hebridean warrior Somerled. Around 1160, Somerled invited Cistercian monks from Armagh to build an abbey by the Allt nam Manach, the 'Stream of the Monks'. Somerled is thought to be buried in the abbey, though no trace of his grave survives. His descendents founded the Lordship of the Isles and gave rise to the Clans MacDougal, MacDonald, MacRory and MacAlister.

A shelter in the abbey grounds is home to a collection of ornately carved late-medieval grave slabs depicting knights, monks, ships, salmon, otters and other images. James IV disbanded the abbey in 1507, and gave its lands to David Hamilton, Bishop of Argyll.

Go back down past the car park, turning right to follow the B842. Cross the bridge over the Saddell Water and take the first left through a stone gateway into the Saddell Estate. A glorious tree-lined driveway leads straight down to Saddell

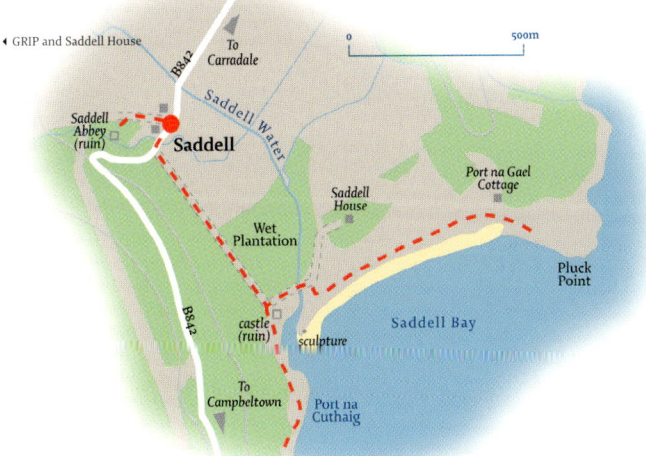

Castle. Hamilton began work on the castle the year after being given the land. A typical towerhouse of the time, it became one of several bastions of the powerful MacDonald family before coming into the possession of Archibald Campbell, 7th Earl of Argyll, in 1607.

Go through the arch to the right to follow the track along the shore. Perched on the rocks, where the Saddell Water flows into the bay, is a strange, lonely figure. This is GRIP, a sculpture by Antony Gormley. It was originally commissioned for just 12 months, as part of the LAND installation to mark the Landmark Trust's 50th anniversary. But thanks to a private donor, it will remain indefinitely.

Return back through the arch to the front of the castle, and bear right. Immediately beyond a bridge over the Saddell Water, turn right to follow a long straight grassy track which runs parallel to the shore.

Saddell House is on the left. The Campbells of Saddell built themselves Saddell House in 1774, and the castle gradually fell into disrepair. Saddell Estate was bought by the Landmark Trust in 1976, who restored the castle and house.

The end of the track swings around to arrive at a cottage, officially called Port na Gael but known affectionately as Mull of Kintyre Cottage, as it featured in the video for the song of the same name by Paul McCartney and Wings. The whole video, which famously depicted the Campbeltown Pipe Band marching along a beach, was filmed here at Saddell Bay, a good 31km away from the Mull of Kintyre.

Retrace your steps to the beginning of the walk, or return along the beach if the mood takes you.

Machrihanish and the Gauldrons

Distance 5.1km **Time** 1 hour 30
Terrain surfaced and unsurfaced tracks, beach; one avoidable incline
Map OS Explorer 356 **Access** bus to Machrihanish from Campbeltown

The dramatic coastline west of Machrihanish has much to explore, with fantastic views across to Rathlin Island and wildlife galore.

From the car park on the seafront at Machrihanish, stride out of the village, keeping the beach on the right. As the road begins to head inland, turn right, following the sign for the Seabird Observatory. Keep right at the next two junctions to pass the Marine Environment Research Laboratory.

Turn right again beyond the Research Laboratory to head for a little shack by the shore, which is the Machrihanish Seabird and Wildlife Observatory. More than 200 species of birds have been recorded here, including such rarities as Leach's petrel, Balearic shearwater, grey phalarope, long-tailed skua and Sabine's gull.

Return to the last junction and climb to the trig point on the low hillock immediately ahead. On a clear day, Rathlin Island, where Robert the Bruce sought refuge in 1306 following defeat at the Battle of Methven, can be seen just off the Northern Irish coast.

Continue down the other side of the hillock to return to the surfaced track. The concrete blocks here are all that remain of a 137m-high tower from which the world's first two-way transatlantic transmission was achieved. For three days in January 1906, Professor Reginald Fessenden sent

Morse code messages to a similar tower near Boston, Massachusetts. Fessenden's experiments were ultimately unsuccessful, and the mast blew down in a storm 11 months later.

At the surfaced track, turn right. The track soon peters out but continue across a flat grassy tract before following the foreshore by a beach. Continue through a gap in a drystane dyke to arrive at the bay known as the Gauldrons.

The towering cliffs at the bay's southern end are a textbook on geology, with obvious layers of mica-schist, Old Red Sandstone and basalt lava. Its Gaelic name is *Innean nan Gailleann*, meaning 'the Bay of Storms'. On a stormy day, this bay is battered by the full force of the Atlantic. The bay was formed by waves wearing away at the soft mica-schist thousands of years ago, causing the upper parts of the cliffs to fall. The debris can still be seen on the beach to this day.

After his encounter with a spider on Rathlin Island, Robert the Bruce crossed to Kintyre, gathered his forces and trained his soldiers near the Gauldrons.

Head back along the beach, through the gap in the dyke and back across the first beach. Here, you can simply return the way you came, or, for an elevated view of the seascape, turn to follow a grassy track uphill. The view is fantastic from the top, with the whole 6km length of Machrihanish Beach visible to the north. Jura and Islay are prominent on the western horizon. Gigha is further north, but closer.

Turn left just before arriving at a gate to follow the fence back towards the sea. Continue along the line of the fence, dropping slowly to meet with the outward track. Follow it back to the Research Station and then retrace your steps back to Machrihanish.

Beinn Ghuilean

Distance 7km **Time** 2 hours 15
Terrain roads, hill tracks, forest tracks;
some steep inclines **Map** OS Explorer 356
Access bus to Campbeltown from
Lochgilphead, Tarbert and Glasgow

The viewpoint at the highest point of this circuit offers sweeping views across the Laggan, the flat triangle of land between Campbeltown, Machrihanish and Westport. Insectivorous butterworts cover the forest floor, while you may also spot buzzards, kestrels and wildfowl.

Beinn Ghuilean dominates the skyline to the south of Campbeltown. The hill's name is derived from the Gaelic word *gualann*, meaning shoulders, and from some angles, the hill does indeed look like a pair of shoulders.

The walk begins at the Old Quay in Campbeltown, opposite the Royal Hotel. Cross the road, passing the hotel, and walk up Main Street. Turn right down Lorne Street, following a sign for Machrihanish, staying on the street as it sweeps left to become Witchburn Road.

Continue along Witchburn Road for 450m, taking the second street on the left, the unsignposted Tomaig Road, and following it out of town. The road narrows as you leave the town, climbing the hill and passing a cemetery.

At a junction, continue straight ahead to go through a gate signposted for the Beinn Ghuilean Trails.

Walk along the vehicle track beyond the gate, going through another gate to pass a reservoir. This is Crosshill Loch. Constructed before 1868, the reservoir provides Campbeltown with its drinking

water. It is also the source of water, via a dedicated supply, for the town's three distilleries: Springbank, Glengyle and Glen Scotia.

Begin to climb again, staying on the main track and passing a Forestry Commission sign for Beinn Ghuilean to enter the woodland. Bear right at a fork to follow a much rougher track leading steeply up the slope, quickly deteriorating into a grassy hill track. As it swings to cross a burn, the summit of Beinn Ghuilean looms above. The track quickly levels out to swing around in a wide semi-circle back towards Campbeltown, arriving at a bench.

The bench offers an excellent view across the reservoir and the road that leads past it. Below, Campbeltown sits in front of Campbeltown Loch, with Davaar Island standing sentinel at its entrance. Beyond, across the Lower Clyde, is the Isle of Arran. The view to the west sweeps across the entire width of the Kintyre peninsula, with Islay on the horizon and the Paps of Jura visible over the hills to the northwest.

Continue downhill to the right of the bench, where a wide grassy track winds down to return to the vehicle track. Go straight across and continue downhill through the trees on the other side, bearing right almost immediately, and ignoring any further tracks to the left or right. After dropping through a number of switchbacks near the bottom of the hill, the track levels out as it arrives beside the reservoir's dam. The 14m-high dam holds back 172 million litres of water.

Cross a bridge over a burn and begin to climb again. Turn right at a crosspaths, going through a gate and following the track back to meet with the outward route. Turn downhill to follow the outward route back to the beginning.

Crosshill Loch from the viewpoint

Davaar Island and the Crucifixion Cave

Distance 6.6km **Time** 1 hour 45 **Terrain** shingle, rocky foreshore and unsurfaced tracks **Map** OS Explorer 356 **Access** no public transport to the start; walk southeast from Campbeltown along the seafront for 3.2km; dogs are not allowed on the island; check tide times

In 1887, some fishermen discovered a painting of the Crucifixion in a cave on Davaar Island, which sits at the mouth of Campbeltown Loch. Tourists and pilgrims flocked in, convinced that a miracle had occurred. The painting can still be seen today, and this short but sometimes challenging walk visits both it and the island's lighthouse.

The island's name is from the Gaelic *Eilean Da Bharr*, meaning 'Double-pointed Island', in reference to the twin prominences visible from the sea side. It is only an island at high tide, being linked to the mainland by An Doirlinn (or the Doirlinn), a 1.3km-long bank of shingle, which is only accessible three hours before and after low tide. The tide comes in quickly, so allow yourself plenty of time to get there and back.

The walk begins in a parking lay-by on Kilkerran Road, 3.2km southeast of Campbeltown. Go through a gate at the western end of the lay-by and follow the short track down to the pebbly beach. Continue straight ahead to follow the Doirlinn towards a navigation beacon, which marks a corner on the sandbank, before swinging towards the island.

Arriving on dry land, turn left to follow a vehicle track around the island's northwestern edge. Pass a couple of holiday cabins to reach Davaar Lighthouse. The lighthouse sits on the island's northeast point, marking the south side of the entrance to

◀ The Crucifixion Cave

Campbeltown Loch. It was built by David and Thomas Stevenson and was completed in 1854 at a cost of between £3000 and £4000. A clockwork mechanism turned a mercury vapour lamp, which flashed every 30 seconds. The lighthouse was automated in 1983, and the lighthouse keeper's cottage is now let out as holiday accommodation.

Return to the end of the Doirlinn, but bear left, following a sign for the Cave Painting, to walk along a grassy track on the southwestern shore. The track deteriorates beyond the ruins of an old cottage. Make your way carefully along the rocky foreshore beneath the cliffs, which are dotted with caves.

The painting is in the seventh cave and is signposted. It was eventually discovered to be the work of Alexander MacKinnon, an art teacher in Campbeltown. He claimed that he had had a dream in which he painted Christ on the cross on the wall of the cave. Working in secret, he painted the scene.

When the story of the painting's true origins came out, MacKinnon was called a fraud, fired from his job and fled to England. However, he returned twice, once in 1902 and again in 1934, to restore his painting, which was deteriorating due to its exposure to the elements. Since his death, it has been the job of the art teachers of Campbeltown Grammar School to maintain it.

Having admired the painting, retrace your steps to the Doirlinn and back to the beginning of the walk.

Glenramskill Old Road

Distance 5.8km **Time** 1 hour 45
Terrain formal and informal roads, hill tracks; moderate ascents
Map OS Explorer 356 **Access** no public transport to the start; walk southeast from Campbeltown along the seafront for 3.2km

The road which runs east, then south around the coast from Glenramskill was built around 1850-53 by the Duke of Argyll and was maintained at the expense of the Kintyre Roads Trustees. It replaced the Old Road, which went up and over the lower slopes of Meall Mor, itself a sub-peak of Beinn Ghuilean. This pleasant circuit follows the Old Road across the headland before returning along the coast via its replacement.

The walk begins in a parking lay-by on Kilkerran Road, 3.2km southeast of Campbeltown. From here, An Doirlinn, the causeway out to Davaar Island, can be seen if the tide is low. The rocks and mudflats around it are popular with local winkle and whelk collectors. Campbeltown Loch is a haven for seabirds, including northern gannet, black-tailed godwit, common tern and common guillemot.

Follow the road back towards Campbeltown, passing a long jetty which extends out into Campbeltown Loch. The jetty serves an Oil Fuel Depot, run on behalf of the MOD by the Oil and Pipelines Agency, who have been providing oil to the Royal Navy since 1986. Deliveries of oil are received at the jetty via ocean-going tankers, and stored in six huge tanks further up the hill.

After 800m, immediately before Glenramskill House, turn left to climb the hill on a rough vehicle track. This is the beginning of the Old Road. Where the

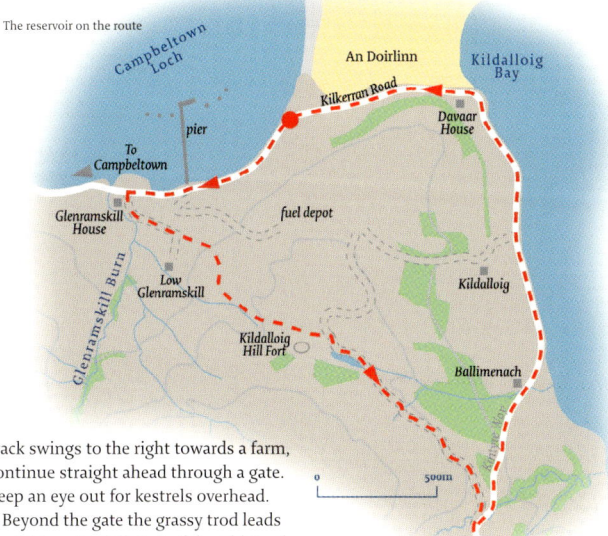

◂ The reservoir on the route

track swings to the right towards a farm, continue straight ahead through a gate. Keep an eye out for kestrels overhead.

Beyond the gate the grassy trod leads straight up the hill. Part of the Old Road has been built over by the tanks of the Oil Fuel Depot straight ahead, so swing to the right just beyond a gate on your left to bypass the depot, paralleling the high fence which surrounds it.

The track pulls away from the fence to go through a gate, climbing straight up the wide shallow ditch that leads up the hill beyond. The hillock to the right as you approach another gate contains the remains of Kildalloig Hill Fort. The name is from the Gaelic *Cill Dallaig*, meaning 'Dalloc's Church', although there is no trace of such a building. The fort was probably constructed during the 2nd or 3rd centuries, and remained in use as late as the 8th century.

Beyond the gate, turn right to join the Old Road again. Pass a small reservoir with an attractive little fishing hut and continue straight ahead through another gate. The track begins to descend, offering superb views towards Davaar Island. The tiny island of Ailsa Craig can be seen on the southeastern horizon, with Arran to the northeast.

The Old Road comes to an end at a junction with a single-track road, 900m after the reservoir. Turn left to join the Kintyre Way and descend to the seafront. Watch out for otters scampering around the shoreline here. Continue along the road to return to the start of the walk.

The Mull of Kintyre

Distance 4.2km **Time** 1 hour 45
Terrain good surfaced but very steep road throughout; brief optional diversion on hill track **Map** OS Explorer 356
Access no public transport to the start

It is virtually impossible to mention the Mull of Kintyre without humming a few bars of Paul McCartney's classic 1977 hit of the same name. But if the mist isn't rolling in from the sea, Rathlin Island and the mountains of County Antrim can be seen from here. Northern Ireland is just 20km away.

Unusually for a hill walk, this very straightforward route starts at the top of a hill, descending 290m to the Mull of Kintyre Lighthouse, which sits 85m above the turbulent waters of the North Channel.

The walk begins at a car park 64m below the summit of Tòrr Mòr, 9km along a single-track road which leaves the B842 at Druma Voulin, west of Southend, and climbs high into the hills at the bottom corner of the Kintyre peninsula.

Beyond the car park, the road is blocked by a wooden gate – walk around it and follow the road as it snakes steeply down the hill. The lighthouse almost immediately comes into view far below.

Reaching a hairpin bend at the end of a long straight section, a stone cairn can be seen on the hill to the right. Take the obvious unsurfaced track which leads up the hill towards it.

In June 1994, in thick fog, a Chinook helicopter crashed into the hillside here, killing all 29 people on board. The cairn is a memorial to the victims, who were

The Mull of Kintyre

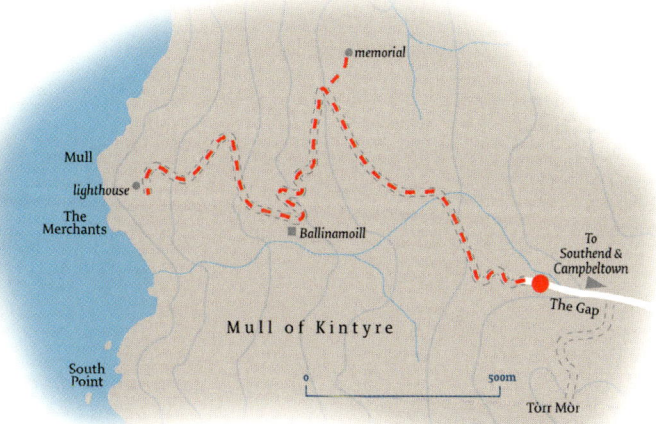

anti-terrorism experts from MI5, the SAS and RUC Special Branch who had been on their way from Northern Ireland to a conference in Inverness.

Return to the road to continue down the hill. Ballinamoill Cottage, a couple of switchbacks further on, was once home to a shepherd who, before the lighthouse was built, kept a lamp burning in the window to warn ships of the perilous rocks below. Today, Ballinamoill has been thoroughly modernised.

Between the cottage and the lighthouse, a series of closely-spaced drystane dykes were built by a former keeper, who was a keen gardener, in an attempt to shelter his vegetable plots from the wild Atlantic winds which batter the coast here.

The road ends at the lighthouse. It was commissioned following an uninterrupted series of storms in 1782. Two fishing boats were wrecked in one night off the Mull of Kintyre, with many lives lost. Thomas Smith was appointed Engineer to the Northern Lighthouse Board in 1787. Smith, assisted by Robert Stevenson, supervised the building of the new lighthouse – one of the first in Scotland.

The inaccessible location of the proposed lighthouse made the construction difficult. Materials were landed by boat 10km away and carried on horseback, one hundredweight per horse, over the hillside – a journey which took a full day. The lighthouse became operational in November 1788.

It was rebuilt in its current form between 1821 and 1830, and a foghorn was added in 1876. It was automated in 1996. The old lighthouse keepers' homes, known as Hector's House and Harvey's House, are now holiday accommodation.

Retrace your steps back up the hill to the beginning of the walk.

◂ Mull of Kintyre Lighthouse

Keil Caves and Dunaverty Rock

Distance 5.7km **Time** 1 hour 30
Terrain roads, beach, unsurfaced tracks; steep climb (which is optional)
Map OS Explorer 356 **Access** bus to Southend from Campbeltown

Southend, at the very southern end of the Kintyre peninsula, offers a host of historic attractions, as well as a sandy beach. This walk links them all.

The route begins at the Keil Point car park, 1.5km west of Southend along the B842. Walk back along the road, turning left through a gate after 100m and immediately left again to explore the Keil Caves.

The caves were occupied since prehistoric times until as recently as the 19th century, when the 1881 Census recorded that two families, the McFees and the McCallums, lived in them with their children. Three of the caves are known as the Great Cave, the Hermit's Cave and the Piper's Cave. According to a local legend, a piper disappeared here one night and the lonely sound of ghostly pipes can sometimes be heard.

Return to the gate, turning left to climb a set of shallow steps to reach a pair of footprints carved into the rock. They are reputed to belong to St Columba, who arrived at Keil from his home in nearby Antrim in 563. The footprint nearest the sea is definitely ancient, but the other one was carved in 1856 by a local stonemason, who also added the incorrect date of 564 between the two. It is thought that the older footprint might have been used in ceremonies to inaugurate kings. There is a similar carved footprint at Dunadd in

KEIL CAVES AND DUNAVERTY ROCK

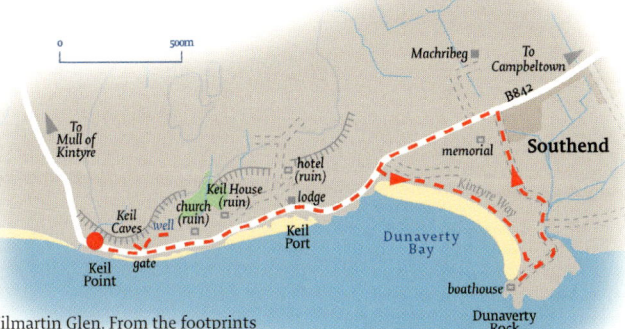

Kilmartin Glen. From the footprints continue along the track to reach the Holy Well, also ascribed to Columba and which is said to have healing properties.

Returning to the gate, continue along the road towards Southend, passing Keil cemetery and the ruins of Keil House, formerly a massive Tudor-style mansion built by a Glasgow cotton merchant who lost his fortune in a banking crash, and the white-walled shell of the five-storey modernist Keil Hotel which closed its doors in 1992.

At a Kintyre Way waymark, turn right through a gate and drop down to the beach. Walk the length of the beach, aiming for a Kintyre Way waymarker at the far end, where a track climbs to join a road. Turn right on to the road to head down to Dunaverty Rock, a wide sea stack on the headland.

The optional track to the summit of Dunaverty Rock is a very steep climb with some scrambling involved, but it is rewarded by spectacular views back across the bay to the start of the walk.

At one time, Dunaverty Castle stood here. After the Battle of Rhunahaorine Moss in 1647, a defeated Royalist army under the command of Archibald MacDonald of Sanda were placed under siege in the castle by a Covenanter Army led by General David Leslie. The Royalists agreed to surrender after the Covenanters captured the castle's water supply, but when they left they were put to the sword at the request of Reverend John Naves and Archibald Campbell, 1st Marquess of Argyll. More than 300 men, women and children were slaughtered.

Returning to the bottom of Dunaverty Rock, follow the Kintyre Way along the road towards Southend, crossing Dunaverty Golf Course. Reaching the B842, turn left. Almost immediately, look out for a memorial to the Dunaverty Massacre in the field to the right. The enclosure is known as the Tomb of the MacDonalds and contains the remains of many of those who died defending 'Blood Rock'. Continue along the road to return to the beginning of the walk.

◀ St Columba's Footprint

The tiny Isle of Gigha, pronounced 'gee-ah', with a hard 'g', is just 11km long and 2.5km wide. It is the most southerly Hebridean island. A ferry crosses the 4.5km from Tayinloan on the Kintyre peninsula in 20 minutes. Ardminish, the only village on the island, is home to the ferry port, as well as the post office, general store and hotel. The entire shoreline is composed of rocky inlets and bays containing white, sandy beaches, although the island is flatter and gentler on its east side than on the craggy west.

Gigha's name derives from the old Norse *Gudey*, meaning 'God's Island' or 'Good Island'. In 1263, the Viking fleet of King Haakon of Norway was anchored here before the Battle of Largs, but there is evidence that Gigha has been occupied for around 5000 years – indeed, most of the walks in this chapter pass close to several prominent prehistoric standing stones.

Until 2002, the entire island was owned by the Holt family. The islanders bought it for £4m in March 2002. Some £3m was raised from trusts and, by 2004, the Isle of Gigha Heritage Trust had raised another £1m to pay off the remainder of the debt.

Although a single-track road runs for the entire length of the island from north to south, all of the routes in this chapter begin at the ferry port at Ardminish. Vehicles can be left at Tayinloan, where there is more space for parking.

Eilean Garbh from the summit of Cnoc nan Gobhar ▶

Isle of Gigha

1 The North End and the Twin Beaches   52
The long walk along Gigha's only road is rewarded with a visit to two of Scotland's most beautiful beaches

2 Creag Bhàn   54
Climb to the highest point on Gigha to drink in the fine views

3 Achamore Gardens and Ardminish   56
Explore the subtropical gardens of Achamore before traversing the hillside above Ardminish

4 Cuddyport Beach   58
Visit evidence of Gigha's industrial past before relaxing on a hidden beach

5 The Bodach and the Cailleach   60
Visit these two mysterious standing stones in a circuit around the southern part of the island

ISLE OF GIGHA

The North End and the Twin Beaches

Distance 16.5km **Time** 4 hours 45
Terrain road for most of the way, good surfaced and unsurfaced paths
Map OS Explorer 357 **Access** bus to Tayinloan from Lochgilphead, Tarbert and Campbeltown, then 20-minute ferry to Ardminish

This is a long walk, but you can take a break in the middle to relax on one of Scotland's best beaches.

From the ferry terminal at Ardminish, saunter up the road to the village, turning right at the post office to follow the sign for Gigha (North). Head along the single-track road, quickly leaving the village behind. After 3km, just beyond Tarbert Farm, a memorial cairn sits on Cnoc an Eireachdais, the 'Hill of the Assembly'.

In December 1991, the Russian factory fishing ship *Kartli* was wrecked near Gigha, killing four crew members. The ship was not salvaged and it sank two years later. The cairn, with the ship's compass embedded in the top, was unveiled on the 25th anniversary of the accident.

In the past, Cnoc an Eireachdais was where the islanders administered justice. Those found guilty were taken a little further north, to a 2m-high, Bronze Age standing stone, called the Giant's Tooth, which still sits by the roadside today. Their heads were placed in the cleft in the middle of the stone and they were left to hang. The stone aligns with the Paps of Jura, and it is thought that its original use was to mark the setting sun of the midsummer solstice.

Continue along the road, turning left at a sign for the Twin Beaches to walk down an unsurfaced track which leads to a

◀ Bàgh na Dòirlinne, the North Beach

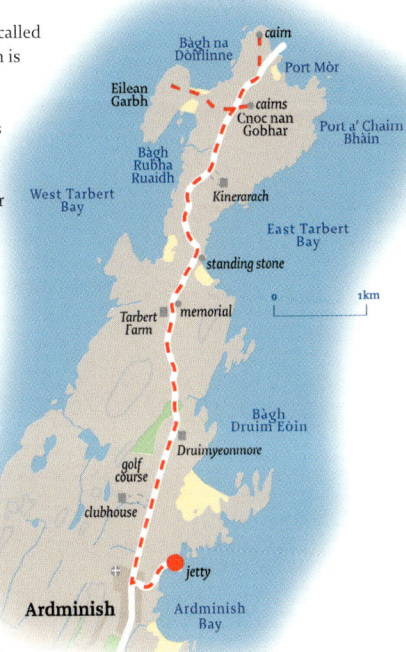

narrow stretch of sandy dunes called a tombolo. The bay to the north is Bàgh na Dòirlinne and to the south is Bàgh Rubha Ruaidh. At the far end of the tombolo is Eilean Garbh, the 'Rough Isle'. A rugged, rocky island, it is barely accessible in the summer due to bracken and briars.

Returning to the road, go straight across, and up a short flight of steps. Turn left by a blue waymark post to climb steeply up to the top of Cnoc nan Gobhar. There are two cairns up here with views over Islay and Jura, and across to the mainland, where West Loch Tarbert slips between Knapdale and Kintyre. Looking south, the view stretches all the way down Gigha to Creag Bhàn.

Walk back to the road again, turning right this time. A little further on, divert left along a vehicle track, crossing a pasture and continuing along a set of wide stepping stones laid across a muddy track through the bracken. The track climbs to the 'Watch Cairn' on the summit of the hill at the far north end of Gigha. The cairn is modern but sits on top of the remains of a prehistoric cist which was removed in the 19th century.

In the past, the cairn was the site of a large fire which was lit to warn the islanders on Jura and Islay when invaders were approaching. More recently, it was used to let the captain of the Islay steamer know when he needed to pick up passengers from Gigha.

Make your way back to the road and head back to the beginning of the walk.

Creag Bhàn

Distance 7.3km **Time** 2 hours 15
Terrain mostly surfaced roads,
unsurfaced hill track to the summit;
moderate ascent **Map** OS Explorer 357
Access bus to Tayinloan from
Lochgilphead, Tarbert and Campbeltown,
then 20-minute ferry to Ardminish

At a lowly 101m, Creag Bhàn is the highest point on Gigha. Nevertheless, the view from the top surpasses that of many a Munro, making the short, easy climb to the summit well worth the minimal effort.

The summit rocks have weathered to a pale grey, giving Creag Bhàn its name, which translates from Gaelic as 'the White Rock'. It is easily spotted from the ferry, a broad rocky hill rising from halfway up the island.

Walk up the hill from the ferry terminal, turning right at the post office in Ardminish. Head out of the village, continuing along the road for 1.6km and passing Gigha Golf Club on the left. In spring and early summer, the roadside here is lined with bluebells, marsh marigolds, primroses, stitchworts, germander speedwell, herb Robert, red campion, celandines and cuckoo pint. Listen out too, for whitethroats, sedge warblers, whinchats, wheatears, wrens and yellowhammers.

Turn left opposite the farm at Druimyeonmore, where two roads, separated by a fence, lead off uphill. Take the left one, crossing a couple of cattle grids to follow a vehicle track which veers first right, then left to gradually climb the hill, finally heading westwards beneath

the slopes of Creag Bhàn.

Keep right at a fork to stay on the main track, turning uphill by a metal utility shed 60m later, where a grassy trod climbs up to the Gigha Service Reservoir. This small covered reservoir is the source of the island's water supply.

Bear right to circumvent the reservoir and continue up the rocky track, looking behind you every so often to enjoy the view back across Mill Loch. The top of the hill is relatively flat, though strewn with boulders and clad with gorse and heather. These rocks were formed around 635 million years ago, when Gigha was near the South Pole. Around 22,000 years ago, during the Late Devensian ice age, they were rounded and worn by southwesterly glacial movement.

Weave your way around and between the boulders along the obvious well-worn track, following the waymarker posts that guide the route to the trig point at the summit. For such a small hill, the view from the top is remarkable. A view indicator near the trig points out Machrihanish, the Mull of Kintyre, the Isle of Cara, Port Ellen and Port Askaig on Islay, Craighouse on Jura, the Paps of Jura, Ben More on Mull, the Gulf of Corryvrekan, Ben Cruachan, West Loch Tarbert, Goat Fell on Arran (behind Kintyre) and Tayinloan. To the southwest, Rathlin Island sits in front of the hills of County Antrim in Northern Ireland.

Closer to hand, the entire island can be seen, from Eilean Garbh and the Twin Beaches to the north to the 'Dancing Ladies' – the local name for the island's wind farm – to the south. Keep an eye on the sky for merlin and buzzards.

From the summit, retrace your steps back down to the ferry terminal.

◂ Mill Loch from the slopes of Creag Bhàn

Achamore Gardens and Ardminish

Distance 4.5km **Time** 1 hour 30 **Terrain** surfaced and unsurfaced tracks, gentle ascent and descent **Map** OS Explorer 357 **Access** buses to Tayinloan from Lochgilphead, Tarbert and Campbeltown, then 20-minute ferry to Ardminish

A renowned collection of azaleas, rhododendrons and camellias, New Zealand tree ferns, hydrangeas and fuchsias make Achamore Gardens an unmissable destination for any visitor to Gigha. It is worth interrupting this circuit, which climbs to the hillside above Ardminish, to thoroughly explore the gardens.

Head uphill from the ferry terminal, bearing left via a kissing gate at the first junction. Cross the field, aiming for a gap in the fence on the far side. At the opposite corner of the next field, climb a stile over the wall.

Turn left to stroll along the single-track road, passing the Gigha Hotel. A few metres beyond Gigha Fire Station, turn right into the trees, immediately bearing left to wander through gentle woodland.

Reaching a road, cross over and go through the visitor entrance to Achamore Gardens. Turn right at a payment booth (entrance fee) to amble up a driveway through formal parkland. Achamore House quickly comes into view.

The house was built in 1884 for Captain William James Scarlett. He planted a mixed woodland around the house to provide cover for game birds, transforming the grounds into a sporting estate.

The estate was redeveloped by Colonel Sir James Horlick in 1944, who spent the profits from his bedtime drink on a world class collection of rhododendrons and camellias, which can still be seen in the gardens today.

Just before reaching the house, keep

Achamore Gardens and Ardminish

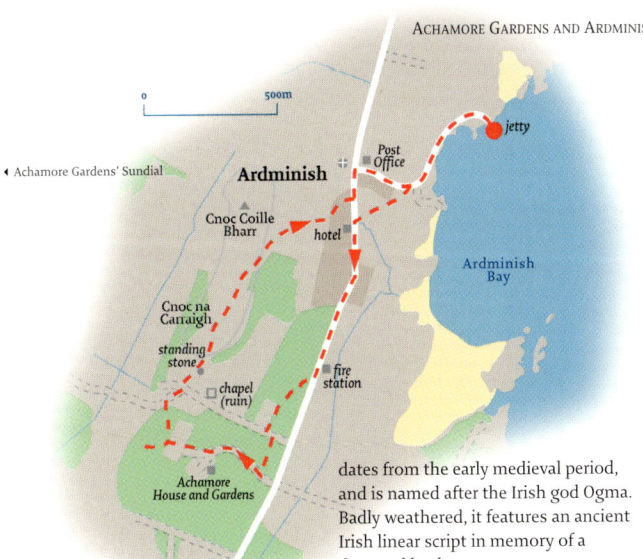

◀ Achamore Gardens' Sundial

right to head behind the public toilets, where a gate leads into a beautifully laid out walled garden. Cross the garden, passing the sundial at the centre, and through the gateway at the far side. Steps opposite lead up to a viewpoint showcasing an impressive panorama across the Sound of Jura to Islay and Jura.

Returning down the steps, turn left at the bottom, ambling beneath a canopy of trees and through a gate to arrive at a road. Turn right, then left at the next junction. Go right again almost immediately, following a sign for the Ogham Stone. Go through a kissing gate, before diverting right to climb up to the stone. This hillock is called Cnoc na Carraigh, the 'Hill of the Pillar'. The stone dates from the early medieval period, and is named after the Irish god Ogma. Badly weathered, it features an ancient Irish linear script in memory of a deceased leader.

Return to continue along the track, ascending gently to traverse open hillside. Creag Bhan can be seen ahead, while the hill slopes down towards the sea on either side. Soon the path, now rough and uneven underfoot, begins to descend, passing through an old gate. When it eventually peters out, continue downwards, aiming for a telegraph pole in the corner of a field.

Keep to the right of the pole, going through a gap in the wall and continuing downhill in the general direction of the swing park behind the Gigha Hotel.

Reaching a fence, turn left. Go through the first gate, shortly arriving back at the road. Turn left to walk back to Ardminish, turning downhill by the post office to return to the ferry terminal.

Cuddyport Beach

Distance 4.5km **Time** 1 hour 30
Terrain surfaced and unsurfaced roads and tracks; some minor scrambling
Map OS Explorer 357 **Access** bus to Tayinloan from Lochgilphead, Tarbert and Campbeltown, then 20-minute ferry to Ardminish

The breathtakingly beautiful sandy bay at Cuddyport is one of Gigha's best-kept secrets. An idyllic spot, much favoured by seabirds, it is a perfect destination on a warm summer's day. This linear walk steps into Gigha's history, incorporating a visit to the remains of a 13th-century chapel and a quernstone quarry.

Head uphill from the ferry terminal, bearing left via a kissing gate by a cairn of painted stones. Cross the field beyond, going through a gap in the fence at the far side. Cross a stile over the wall at the far corner of the next field, and turn left to drop downhill on the road past the Gigha Hotel. Just beyond Gigha Fire Station, take the path into the trees, bearing left almost immediately to wander through the woods to a road.

Turn right here, passing the village hall, and climbing gently to pass the ruins of Kilchattan Chapel. The chapel dates from the 13th century, and is dedicated to St Cathan, a 6th-century Irish missionary who based himself on Bute and who spread the gospel throughout Kintyre and the Western Isles. It was in use until the early 18th century, when it was replaced by a new church opposite the current hotel. The ruins were conserved and

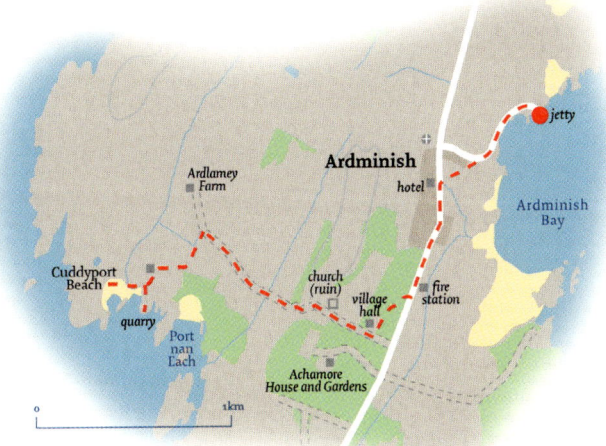

consolidated in 2010, with stainless steel ties added through the north and south walls to make the ruin safe.

Follow the main track to pass a house and go round the bend, then continue along the access track to Ardlamey Farm. Before you reach the farm, turn left to walk along the edge of a field, passing through a gap in the drystane dyke, then cross the next field towards a gate at the far side.

Turn right immediately before the gate, following the fence to reach another gate by a cottage. Go through this gate, and the one immediately beyond, following a sign for Cuddyport Beach and Quernstone Quarry. This leads you down a grassy track towards the sea.

Reaching a fork, bear left, then stay right to cross the headland. Near the far end, look out for circular marks cut into the rock. There are several locations in the southwest of Gigha where quernstones were quarried, and this one is perhaps the best example. Quernstones (corn stones) were used for grinding grain. More than 100 stones were quarried here, then transported by boat. The finished stones were around 50cm in diameter, and were used to grind grain by hand rather than in a mill. The quarry probably dates from the 18th century.

Return to the fork and bear left along the other path, dropping down to cross a stile to reach Cuddyport Beach. This beach, which also goes by the name of Port an t-Samhlaidh, the Bay of the Spectre, is one of Gigha's more secluded beaches. The old stone pier at the far side of the bay was where the quernstones were loaded for onward transportation.

Having enjoyed the beach, retrace your steps back to the beginning of the walk.

◀ Kilchattan Church

The Bodach and the Cailleach

Distance 8.7km **Time** 2 hours 30
Terrain surfaced and unsurfaced paths and roads; some minor ascents
Map OS Explorer 357 **Access** bus to Tayinloan from Lochgilphead, Tarbert and Campbeltown, then 20-minute ferry to Ardminish

Through the ages, two ancient standing stones have stood vigil over Gigha, linking today's thriving island with the pagan traditions of old. This circuit checks in at the mysterious stones before visiting one of Gigha's most beautiful beaches.

Head uphill from the ferry terminal, bearing left through a kissing gate by a cairn of painted stones. Cross the field, aiming for a gap in the fence, then walk towards the corner of the next field, where a stile will take you over the wall and onto the road.

Turn left to pass the Gigha Hotel. Just beyond the fire station, turn right into woodland, bearing immediately left to meander along a surfaced path through the trees.

Reaching a road, turn right, passing the village hall and climbing to pass the ruins of Kilchatten Church. The 13th-century church is dedicated to St Cathan, a 6th-century Irish missionary who spread the gospel throughout Kintyre and the Western Isles from his base in Bute.

Bear left as the road crests the hill. Shortly before a cattle grid, bear left through a gate to follow a surfaced path which runs south, offering excellent views across the Sound of Jura to Islay.

After passing through three more gates, look out for a couple of standing stones on top of the small hill known as Cnoc a Shevis. These are the Bodach and the Cailleach. They were regarded in the old days as having mysterious powers. The Bodach, the taller of the two, represented an old man and the smaller, flat-topped Cailleach, an old woman.

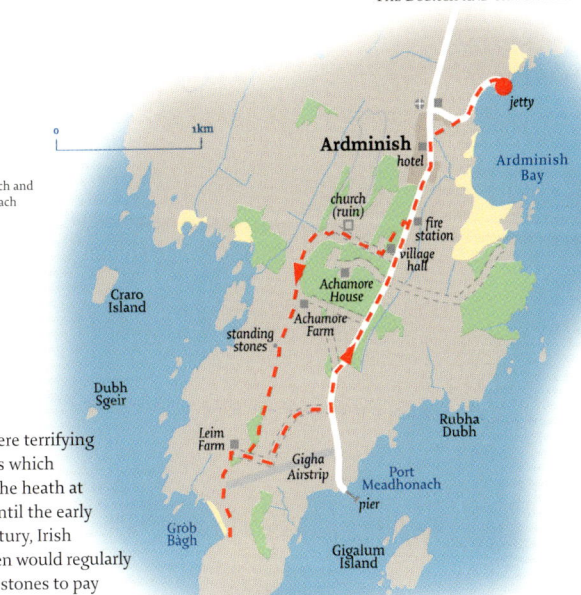

◀ The Bodach and the Cailleach

These were terrifying creatures which walked the heath at night. Until the early 19th century, Irish fishermen would regularly visit the stones to pay homage and to leave offerings.

The stones are said to guarantee Gigha's continuing fertility and prosperity, and bad luck will descend on the island if the stones were to fall, so islanders always ensure that the stones are righted promptly if they show signs of collapse.

Walk along the path, passing beneath a couple of wind turbines and through two more gates, continuing straight ahead to enter woodland. In the spring, the forest floor is carpeted with bluebells.

Beyond the path's final gate, turn right on an unsurfaced vehicle track, bearing left at the top and following a sign for 'The Beach'.

After passing through a further gate, head across a field, bearing right just before another gate to drop down to Leim Beach, one of Gigha's best beaches. The beach sits on Gròb Bagh, the Bay of the Point of Rock, named after the rocky outcrop just offshore. On a clear day, the waters of the bay are turquoise and the beach offers great views towards Islay and Northern Ireland.

Return to the unsurfaced vehicle track, and drop downhill, passing the runway of Gigha Airstrip.

At the bottom of the hill, turn left and follow the road back to Ardminish, turning right across the stile just past the hotel to return to the ferry terminal.

The Isle of Bute is separated from Cowal by the Kyles of Bute, a narrow but incredibly scenic sea passage at the northern end of the island. The island's name is thought to derive from the Old Irish *bot*, meaning 'fire', in reference to the beacons that Norse settlers lit on the hills.

Bute was first settled in Neolithic times and has been inhabited ever since. The main settlement on the island is the seaside resort of Rothesay. Easily accessible from Scotland's Central Belt, it is still a popular destination for daytrippers, as it has been for well over a century. But it's well worth getting out of the town to experience the real Bute, with a myriad of beaches, prehistoric standing stones and burial sites, seats of Celtic Christianity and scenic gems.

The West Island Way makes its way up the entire length of Bute. Several of the walks in this chapter make use of sections of the route.

At 24km long and between 5 and 8km wide, the island is the second largest in the Clyde Estuary after Arran. It is an island of two halves because it sits astride the Highland Boundary Fault. Loch Fad, which almost splits the island in two, marks the boundary between the lower southern part and the hillier northern end. The western side of the island has a number of safe, sandy beaches with fine views across to the rugged mountains of Arran. The beaches are fantastic places to relax after a day's hiking and perhaps watch the sun go down.

▶ Arran from Scalpsie Bay

Isle of Bute

1 Balnakailly Loop — 64
This wooded circuit at the northern end of the island climbs to a viewpoint across the Kyles of Bute to Cowal

2 Cairn Bàn and St Michael's Grave — 66
Explore the prehistory of Bute in this simple coastal walk

3 The Tramway Trail — 68
Walk from one side of the island to the other along the route of an old tramway

4 Rothesay to Port Bannatyne — 70
Beginning at the ferry terminal, cross the hillside to Port Bannatyne, returning along the coastal road

5 Canada Hill — 72
This viewpoint offered a last poignant sight of relatives heading for a new life in Canada

6 Barone Hill — 74
This hill on the edge of the Highland Boundary Fault was once crowned by an Iron Age fort

7 Stravanan Bay from Kilchattan Bay — 76
Cross from coast to coast in the southern part of the island

8 St Blane's and Kilchattan Bay — 78
Follow the first section of the West Island Way around the southern tip of Bute

Balnakailly Loop

Distance 6.2km **Time** 2 hours
Terrain unsurfaced tracks, forest vehicle tracks; moderate ascent
Map OS Explorer 362 **Access** bus to Rhubodach from Rothesay; ferry from Colintraive

Climb through an historic oakwood to an abandoned settlement before arriving at a fabulous viewpoint above the Kyles of Bute in this circular walk.

The oakwood was once part of the Forest of Bute, a royal hunting forest in the 15th century. It is home to woodland birds such as redstart, tree pipit, wood warbler, great spotted woodpecker, and spotted and pied flycatcher. There are also over 300 species of mosses, liverworts and lichens, as well as some rare ferns.

The walk begins at the small car park beside the ferry terminal at Rhubodach (from the Gaelic *Rudha-Mhodach*, meaning 'Bute Point'). Continue past the ferry terminal and through a gate, following the sign for the Balnakailly Loop.

The track follows the shore for a little before petering out, but carry on across the pasture, aiming for a gate and another sign at the entrance to the oakwood.

Beyond the gate, cross a wooden bridge over the Balnakailly Burn and wander gradually uphill through the trees, following the burn along a pleasant, if occasionally muddy, woodland track. Soon the track climbs away from the burn. Pass a couple of white-banded waymark posts and enter a commercial Sitka spruce plantation, quickly emerging again at the remains of an old settlement.

There are records of Balnakailly from as early as 1590, though the surviving structures – five buildings, a garden and an enclosure – date from much later. The name of Balnakailly is derived from the

BALNAKAILLY LOOP

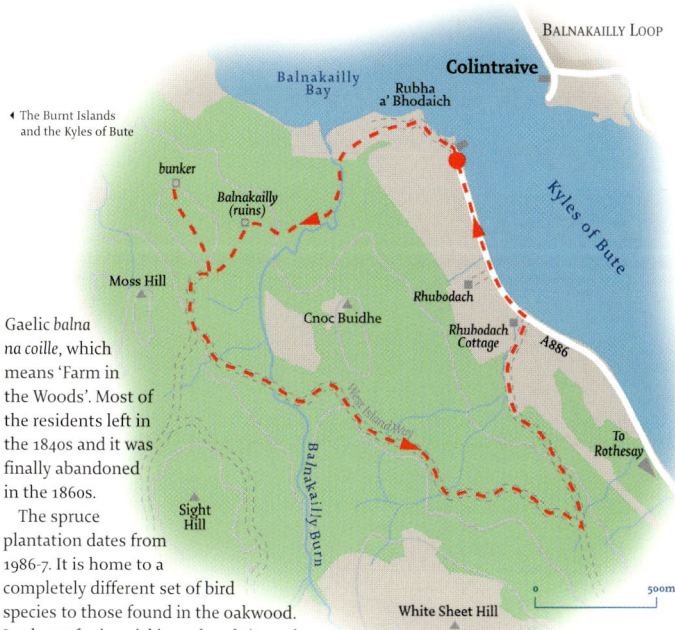

◀ The Burnt Islands and the Kyles of Bute

Gaelic *balna na coille*, which means 'Farm in the Woods'. Most of the residents left in the 1840s and it was finally abandoned in the 1860s.

The spruce plantation dates from 1986-7. It is home to a completely different set of bird species to those found in the oakwood. Look out for jay, siskin and coal tit. In the summer, the woods are filled with the song of the willow warbler, and crossbills forage for pinecones in the treetops.

Continue up the track for 200m to reach the end of a forest vehicle track. Turn right immediately along a path signposted for a Second World War bunker, and follow it to a bench which offers stunning views across the Burnt Islands and the Kyles of Bute to the hills of Cowal.

A few metres downhill, an old military bunker can be seen. This was used as a control centre for simulation of bomb drops of German Pathfinder squadrons. Nearby, towers topped with fuel tanks were built to resemble rows of buildings. When the fuel was set alight, it appeared that the buildings had suffered a direct hit. This in turn would draw in enemy bombers, fooled into thinking that they were bombing the nearby naval installations at Rothesay and Port Bannatyne. Despite this subterfuge, the forest was never bombed.

Returning to the vehicle track, follow it to a junction. Turn left to meander through the trees, turning left at another junction and following the sign for the Balnakailly Loop. Arriving at the road by the shore, turn back towards the ferry terminal and the end of the walk.

Cairn Bàn and St Michael's Grave

Distance 7.6km **Time** 2 hours 15
Terrain rough vehicle track, woodland tracks and fields; steep ascents
Map OS Explorer 362 **Access** no public transport to the start

This is a straightforward out-and-back walk with a number of diversions to some of Bute's historic and prehistoric sites. Any or all of them may be ignored if you want to avoid hills or muddy fields, leaving a pleasant level walk along the island's northwest coast.

This corner of Bute was important to the Neolithic farmers who introduced agriculture and pottery to the island. This walk visits three of the many chambered cairns that they left scattered across the island, along with an early Christian chapel and an old ferry port.

The walk begins in the car park at Glecknabae, at the end of the single-track road that leads north from Ettrick Bay. Walk along the private road that continues north along the coast. After 300m, turn right uphill on the signposted Alternative Path to Cairnbaan.

The track quickly fades out beyond a gate, but continue diagonally uphill, heading through another gate, across the pasture beyond and through a third gate beside a clump of trees.

Cross a footbridge to enter an open woodland which, in the late spring, is carpeted with bluebells. Turn right up a forest track beside a burn, which tumbles down over a series of pretty waterfalls. Near the top of the hill, the track swings over another bridge to reach the 30m-long Cairn Bàn (translating from the Gaelic for 'White Cairn'). It is thought to date from 4500-2200BC.

CAIRN BÀN AND ST MICHAEL'S GRAVE

◀ Glenvoidean Cairn

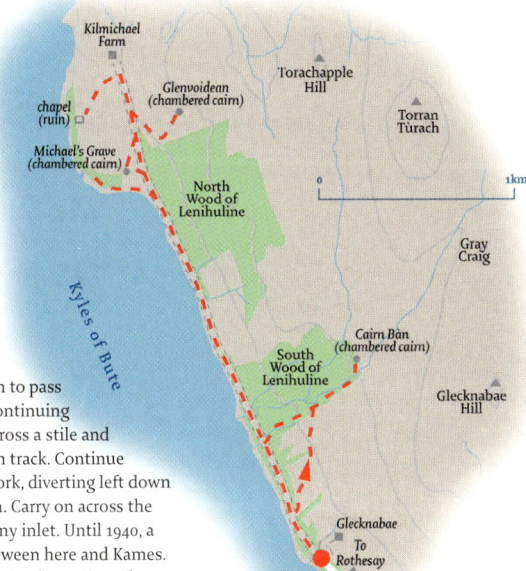

Head back down to pass the first bridge, continuing down the hill to cross a stile and return to the main track. Continue northwards to a fork, diverting left down to a shingle beach. Carry on across the rocks to reach a tiny inlet. Until 1940, a ferry operated between here and Kames.

Returning to the track, continue for 120m before turning left through a gate and crossing the field to reach the cluster of upright stones known as St Michael's Grave. The cairn is thought to date from 3000-2000BC and has no known connection with St Michael.

Walk back to the track through a gate in the northeast corner of the field, and continue past a cottage. Following a sign for Glenvoidean, bear right around the back of the cottage. The track swings northwards before fading out, but head up the steep hill, to reach the two upright stones of Glenvoidean, dating from around 3000BC. It was reused during the Bronze Age and again in medieval times when it served as a corn kiln.

Returning to the main track, bear right. At a sign for St Michael's Chapel, turn left to cross a field. Go through another gate on the far side of the field, and walk over to a circular drystane enclosure which surrounds St Michael's Chapel.

The chapel dates from between the 4th and 7th centuries, and is thought to have been dedicated to St Maccaile, a disciple of St Patrick who died around 488AD.

From the chapel, return to the track and follow it back to the car park.

The Tramway Trail

Distance 9.1km **Time** 2 hours 30
Terrain surfaced tracks and pavements; unsurfaced woodland tracks
Map OS Explorer 362 **Access** bus to Ettrick Bay from Rhubodach, Rothesay and Kilchattan Bay

The only tramway on a Scottish island ran from Rothesay Esplanade to Ettrick Bay via Port Bannatyne.

The Rothesay Tramways Company began a horse-drawn tram service between Rothesay and Port Bannatyne in 1882. The company was bought by British Electric Traction in 1901, who electrified the line and extended it to Ettrick Bay in 1905. It quickly became a popular way for Glasgow daytrippers to reach Ettrick Bay after arriving on the steamship at Rothesay or Port Bannatyne. The trams ran until 1936, when they were superseded by a bus service. The beach at Ettrick Bay is still popular with visitors and locals today, who enjoy paddling in its beautiful, clear waters.

This easy walk begins in front of the Ettrick Bay Tearoom and follows the former tramline across the isthmus between Ettrick Bay and Port Bannatyne.

Go through the entrance to the tearoom's car park, exiting through the gateway directly ahead. The well-maintained track runs parallel to the road and is easy to follow, with no diversions. Pass the cottage of the Etterick Smiddy on the other side of the road, a 19th-century blacksmith's house and workshop which retains its original internal features, including a working bellow and an anvil.

As you pass the next cottage you will

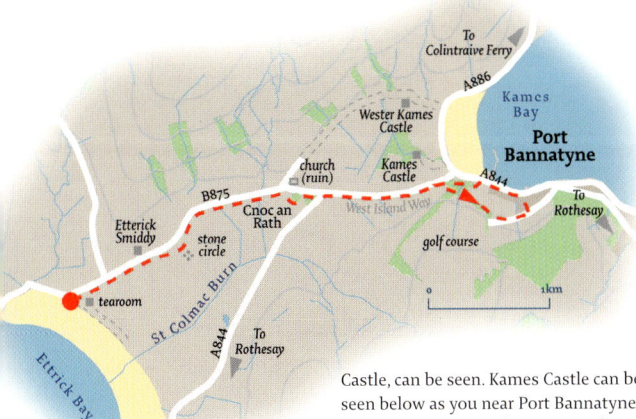

see St Colmac's Stone Circle in the field to the right. One of two stone circles on Bute, the purpose of this 4000-year-old monument is unknown. The roofless shell of St Colmac's Church is across the road from a bend in the track. It was built in 1836 by the second Marquess of Bute as a Gaelic church, but became North Bute Parish Church in 1844. It closed in 1980.

The path doglegs around a tree-covered earthwork named Cnoc an Rath. It has been speculated that this was a fort, a henge or an early medieval ring fort. At the centre of the site is the tomb of James Hamilton of Kames (1775-1849).

Reaching a road, cross over and continue along the pavement, following the sign for Rothesay. On the hillside to the north, the towerhouse, Wester Kames Castle, can be seen. Kames Castle can be seen below as you near Port Bannatyne. This towerhouse was home to Lord Bannatyne, who designed the village, which he called Kamesburgh as an alternative to Rothesay in 1801. It was renamed Port Bannatyne in his honour in 1860.

Turn right into the trees by a West Island Way waymarker. Bear right along a pleasant woodland walkway, quickly emerging onto Bannatyne Mains Road. Take the first left onto Bute Terrace and go down the steps to Quay Street and the seafront. Pass the marina opposite the boatyard. Boat building grew to become an important local industry in the early 20th century.

Turn left on a path between a toilet block and a pétanque pitch. Follow the path into the trees, shortly joining the outward route and following it back to the beginning of the walk.

◂ Ettrick Beach

Rothesay to Port Bannatyne

Distance 9.3km **Time** 2 hours 30
Terrain mostly roads and surfaced paths, some unsurfaced tracks; steep ascents
Map OS Explorer 362 **Access** bus to Rothesay from Rhubodach, Kilchattan Bay and Ettrick Bay; ferry to Rothesay from Wemyss Bay

After an initial steep climb out of Rothesay, this becomes a pleasant upland country walk before dropping down to Port Bannatyne and returning along the seafront.

Begin outside the Victorian Toilets, by the ferry terminal in Rothesay. These ornate public toilets, with their decorated tiles, mosaic floors, imitation marble and glass cisterns, were built in 1899 for use by men only. Modern facilities for women were added in the 1990s.

Walk along the Esplanade, passing the pavilion of the Winter Garden, now known as The Discovery Centre. The Winter Garden was built as a concert hall in 1923-4, and in its heyday was one of Scotland's most famous music halls. Restored in the 1980s, it is now home to exhibitions, amusements and multi-media displays about the history of Bute and its inhabitants, known as 'Brandanes'.

Follow the raised path on the left over the wall and just past the fountain. Cross Argyle Street at the zebra crossing here and turn right, crossing Gallowgate and taking the next left to head up the narrow Chapelhill Road.

As the road veers right, pass the former Free Church Chapel, built for Gaelic speakers in 1860 after their own church converted to delivering sermons in English in 1858.

Turn left to ascend a long flight of steps,

ROTHESAY TO PORT BANNATYNE

turning right onto Westland Road at the top. This is the first of several excellent vantage points on the route, offering views across Rothesay Bay to the Cowal peninsula. Westland Road leads to the westernmost lands owned by the Royal Burgh of Rothesay. Westland Farm has stood at the very end of the road since medieval times.

Follow the West Island Way along Westland Road. The West Island Way, which opened in September 2000, was the first waymarked long-distance footpath on a Scottish island. Swinging briefly north, the mountains of Cowal can be seen straight ahead before the road continues westwards again.

Some 150m before reaching Westland Farm, head along a farm track to the right, waymarked for the West Island Way. This attractive tree-lined track leads through gates in two deer fences. The area between the deer fences has been planted with rowan, hawthorn, ash, willow, oak, alder and some other native species by the Bute Estate.

Leave the West Island Way after the second gate to continue straight ahead along an aggregate surfaced road which drops down towards Port Bannatyne, offering fantastic views across Kames Bay.

Reaching a junction at the bottom of the hill, turn left to walk along a tree-lined vehicle track. At the end of the track, zigzag down to the seafront, turning right to pass the remains of the Old Steamer Pier. The pier was constructed in 1857 to accommodate visiting paddle steamers bringing daytrippers in from Glasgow.

Rounding Ardbeg Point, look out for the ornate marble Thomson Drinking Fountain, which dates from 1867, at the junction with Ardbeg Road. There is an identical one in George Square, Glasgow.

Continue along the seafront to return to the beginning of the walk.

◀ The old steamer pier at Port Bannatyne

Canada Hill

Distance 5.4km **Time** 1 hour 45
Terrain good surfaced and unsurfaced tracks and roads throughout; some steep ups and downs **Map** OS Explorer 362
Access bus to Rothesay from Rhubodach, Kilchattan Bay and Ettrick Bay; ferry to Rothesay from Wemyss Bay

In the first 60 years of the 20th century, nearly 600,000 Scots emigrated to Canada in search of employment opportunities in the New World. Most left Scotland from Glasgow. The friends and family that they left behind would gather on Common Hill (known locally as Canada Hill) above Rothesay to bid one last farewell to their loved ones as they sailed down the Clyde and across the Atlantic. This walk visits the top of the hill before exploring a delightful woodland.

Beginning at the ferry terminal in Rothesay, cross Argyle Street and stroll up the High Street to Rothesay Castle. The castle dates back to Viking times, and has been held by various forces over the centuries, including the Vikings, the Scots and the English. During the War of the Three Kingdoms, Oliver Cromwell installed a garrison here. The castle was destroyed when the garrison was withdrawn, but it has been restored by successive Marquesses of Bute.

Turn left down Castle Street and continue straight ahead at the junction to snake uphill on the appropriately named Serpentine Road, or simply the Serpentine. This remarkable road climbs steeply out of Rothesay through a total of 14 hairpin bends, climbing 70m in a very short distance. Steps connecting the bends in the road make the climb faster but steeper.

Eventually the road straightens out, but continues climbing. As it levels out, carry

◀ The Firth of Clyde

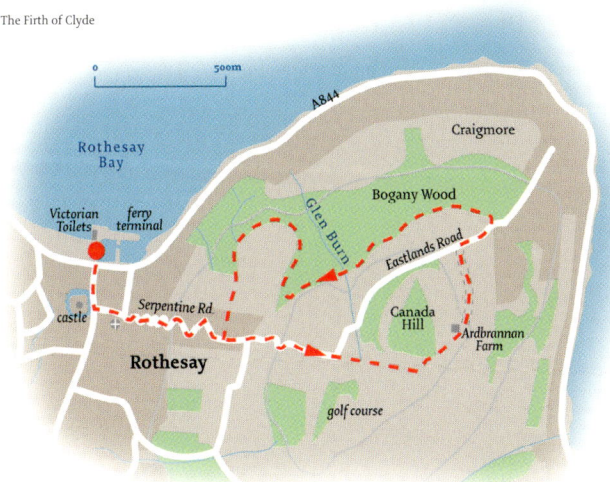

straight on over a staggered junction. Where the road swings sharply to the left, walk straight ahead through a gate to amble uphill along the edge of Rothesay Golf Course, enjoying the view southwest across Loch Ascog and over towards distant Arran. Look out for the trig point on the left beside one of the greens.

Carry on up and over the top of the hill. A view indicator as you descend points out the Ayrshire coast and Cumbrae islands which can be seen across the Firth of Clyde. Drop down to where a bench offers a clearer view across the Clyde. It was here that families gathered to catch a final glimpse of their relatives as they departed in search of a better life.

Swing left by the bench to drop downhill, continuing straight ahead through a gate to head briefly through a riding centre and onto the long drive that leads up to it. Follow the drive to its end, turning right onto the road that you left earlier to continue downhill. The road swings briefly left, then right again. Turn left here, to saunter along a well-defined woodland track beneath a canopy of beech trees. As the track swings down towards the sea, Rothesay and Port Bannatyne can be seen below, with the hills of Cowal in the distance.

After rambling through the undulating woodland for 1.6km, the track climbs to go through a gate. Turn immediately right to skirt along the edge of a field, exiting through another gate, where a short road leads to the top of the Serpentine. Turn downhill to return to the start of the walk.

Barone Hill

Distance 5.9km **Time** 2 hours
Terrain surfaced roads and tracks, hill tracks; moderate ascent
Map OS Explorer 362 **Access** bus to Rothesay from Rhubodach, Kilchattan Bay and Ettrick Bay; ferry to Rothesay from Wemyss Bay

This route climbs to the summit of the small but distinctive Barone Hill, which sits behind Rothesay. The hill's name is derived from the Brythonic *bryn*, meaning 'brow'. It sits immediately north of the Highland Boundary Fault which splits Bute in two and which separates the Scottish Highlands from the Lowlands. Loch Fad, at the foot of the hill, lies in the fault itself.

The walk begins at the Isle of Bute Shinty Club at the end of Meadows Road in Rothesay. Take the track directly opposite the clubhouse, walking parallel to a wall.

At the end of the track, climb the steps, turning right onto another path, which runs alongside a water cut created by the civil engineer Robert Thom in the early 19th century to increase power to the Rothesay Cotton Mill. This brought economic success, and Thom was made Laird of Ascog as a result.

Beyond a gate, turn left onto a road. Turn right in just under 500m, continuing up the hill, passing through two gates and turning right where the track meets a road. Turn right again after 100m, following a muddy track up the hill through long grass and occasional sparse gorse bushes.

Climb over a drystane dyke via a ladder stile and turn immediately right to follow the wall uphill to the summit of Barone Hill. The summit is a panoramic viewpoint with an outlook across much of Bute. The view east is to the mainland and the coast of Inverclyde, while to the

BARONE HILL

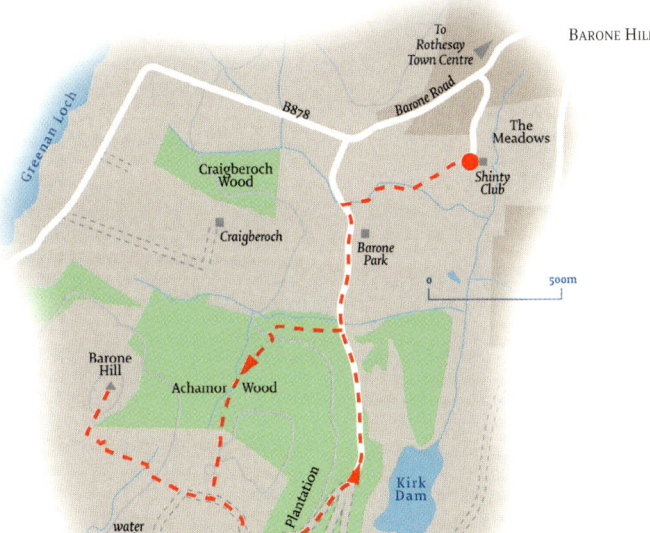

west Arran and Cowal can be seen, with the Kintyre coastline in the distance. Loch Fad is below to the southeast, Greenan Loch to the northwest and Loch Dhu to the southwest.

This summit was once crowned by an Iron Age hillfort, which would have been visible from much of Bute and the seas beyond, and which would have had an imposing presence. Oval shaped, 62m long by 42m wide, and with walls up to 3m thick, it offered a place of refuge for the citizens of Bute in times of trouble.

One such time was in 1334, when Sir Adam Lisle, who governed Bute on behalf of Edward Balliol, son of John Balliol, faced an uprising by the men of Bute, known as the Brandanes (just as people from Bute are known today).

The poorly armed Brandanes were no match for Lisle's well-trained forces and beat a hasty retreat to the now ruined fort. When Lisle's forces pursued them up the hill, the Brandanes rained rocks down on them, killing many of Lisle's soldiers. Taking up the swords of the slain, the Brandanes pursued the survivors, engaging in battle on the plains beneath the hill. The Brandanes won the battle, and Lisle's head was presented to the High Steward, Robert Stewart, the future King Robert II.

Return over the ladder stile and back down the hill, turning left onto the road and following it down to a junction. Turn left here, soon joining the outward route and following this back to the start.

◀ One of the locals relaxes beneath Barone Hill

Stravanan Bay from Kilchattan Bay

Distance 8.4km **Time** 2 hours 15 **Terrain** surfaced and unsurfaced tracks, country roads **Map** OS Explorer 362 **Access** bus to Kilchattan Bay from Rhubodach and Ettrick Bay via Rothesay

This easy walk crosses from one side of Bute to the other on a narrow isthmus at the southern end of the island.

Kilchattan Bay is named after St Cathan, who established a hermitage here in 539. Until the 19th century, it was little more than a few fishermen's cottages.

Head north from the parking area by the bus terminus at the southern end of Kilchattan Bay. The old stone pier was built in 1822 to land coal and other local essentials. Its importance to the local economy grew when the Marquis of Bute established a tile and brickworks in the village in 1849. By the beginning of the 20th century, steamships were bringing tourists. Look out for a wrought-iron weather vane by the pier.

A little beyond a bus stop, turn left uphill between two modern houses, turning right at the top to follow the West Island Way. At the end of the track, turn left through a gate to follow a surfaced track at the edge of some woodland.

Arriving at a road, cross and continue straight ahead, traversing the edge of a field. Cut through another gate and over a small bridge to stroll along the edge of Bute Airfield. The 'runway', a flat grassy strip of land, is behind to your right.

After crossing another field you find yourself heading along the edge of a golf

STRAVANAN BAY FROM KILCHATTAN BAY

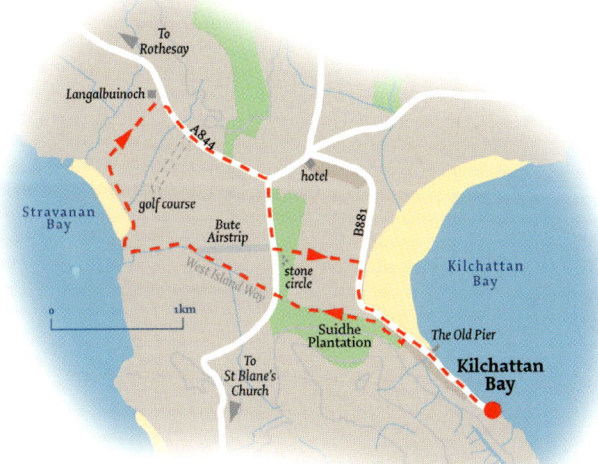

course. Bute Golf Club is a nine-hole golf course. Founded in 1888, it is the oldest golf club on the island. Although you are mostly protected from stray golf balls by thick gorse bushes, the track strays near the greens in a couple of places, and care should be taken.

Turn right at a low wall, following a West Island Way sign. Go through a gap in the wall beyond a small hut, which circumnavigates a green to reach another signpost by a gate.

Leave the golf course by the gate and wander along the shore. This is the remote sand and shingle Langalbuinoch Beach at Stravanan Bay.

Hop over a couple of burns before swinging inland through a gateway at another West Island Way signpost, and walk up a farm vehicle track between two fields. Passing the farm, continue along the farm track, emerging several metres later onto a road.

Part company with the West Island Way here, turning right to walk along the road. Turn right again at a sign for St Blane's Chapel, named after St Cathan's nephew. After a while, head left down a potholed road signposted for the Black Park Standing Stones. Also known as the Kingarth Standing Stones, these were part of a Bronze Age stone circle. Only three of the original seven stones remain. Look out for historical graffiti on the southernmost stone, including a small incised cross.

Continuing down the road, go through another gate and along the side of a couple of fields. Emerge onto a road by the sea, turning right to stroll back along the seafront to Kilchattan Bay.

◂ Kingarth Stone Circle

St Blane's and Kilchattan Bay

Distance 9km **Time** 3 hours
Terrain mostly unsurfaced tracks, some very rocky underfoot; some steep ascents
Map OS Explorer 362 **Access** no public transport to the start; bus from Rothesay to Kilchattan Bay on the route

This varied walk takes in both a hilltop and coastal walking. It includes an important site of early Christianity and a 20th-century lighthouse. The whole route follows the West Island Way.

The walk begins at the small parking area for St Blane's Church at the southern end of Plan Road. Head up the hill towards the church (signposted). Saint Cathan is thought to have established a 6th-century monastery here, although this site is named after his nephew, Saint Blane. It was destroyed by the Vikings around 800. The church dates from the 12th century.

Beyond the church, go through the gap in the wall on the other side. After a gate, turn left to skirt around the hill. Beyond another gate, turn left uphill to join a surfaced track. As you reach the top of the hill there are spectacular views down to the beach at Stravanan Bay and up Bute's west coast. Turn right at another gate, dropping down towards the bottom left corner of the field, before striding uphill again beside a fence. Veer right to follow the fence to a stile.

Do not cross the stile. Instead, turn left to climb steeply to the summit of Suidhe Chatain (or Catan's Hill), crossing another stile to reach the trig point. Both sides of the island can be seen from here.

Return to the first stile and cross it, swinging left to descend by a drystane dyke before passing through a gate and into woodland. Wooden steps lead down into Kilchattan Bay. Turn right at the

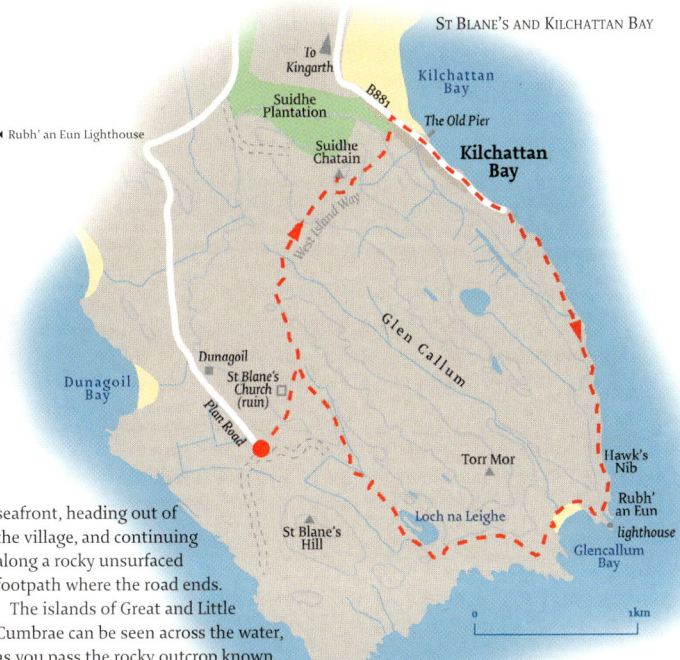

seafront, heading out of the village, and continuing along a rocky unsurfaced footpath where the road ends.

The islands of Great and Little Cumbrae can be seen across the water, as you pass the rocky outcrop known as Hawk's Nib. Continuing south and rounding a corner, the Rubh' an Eun Lighthouse comes into view on a rocky headland at the eastern end of Glencallum Bay.

The 8m-high lighthouse, which faces Little Cumbrae Lighthouse across the Firth of Clyde, was commissioned in 1911 by the Clyde Lighthouses Trust. It stands on the site of an earlier lighthouse, built in the 1880s.

The path around the grey slate beach at Glencallum Bay is strewn with boulders and can be difficult to follow in places. Zigzag up the hill at the far end of the bay, before traversing the hillside towards another waymarker on the horizon.

Soon, swing inland to pass Loch na Leighe, a lochan in the hollow below. Ascending gently and approaching a fence, turn sharply right, following the sign for St Blane's Church.

Reaching a junction, turn left at a waymarker to climb gently uphill by a fence. Continue along a narrow passage between a drystane dyke and a fence. Nip through a gate in the wall and head back to St Blane's Church, before following the outward route to the start.

Cowal gets its name from Comhghall, a leader of one of the four chief tribes of Dal Riata. Comhghall's father, Eric, was a leader of the Scotti who came from Ireland in around 300AD. He is thought to be the Old King Cole of nursery rhyme fame.

The coastline is complicated: four peninsulas stretch from north to south like the thumb and fingers of a giant hand poised to pick up the Isle of Bute. The sea lochs which separate the peninsulas were traditionally used for communication between the different parts of Cowal, but the area is now well-served by road. This quiet backwater, wild like the Hebrides, yet only a couple of hours' drive from Glasgow (or even less time by ferry to Dunoon), is marketed as 'Argyll's Secret Coast'. It is home to eagles, deer and otters, and you might even catch a glimpse of a basking shark.

The villages of the Cowal coast formed part of the 'Glasgow Riviera', where holidaymakers and daytrippers from Glasgow would arrive by paddle steamer on a trip 'doon the watter'. In the early 20th century, Captain Peter 'Para Handy' MacFarlane navigated his coastal puffer *The Vital Spark* around these shores in a series of stories by Neil Munro, published in the *Glasgow Evening News*.

The Cowal Coast

1. **Otter Ferry and the Ballimore Estate** 82
A short and easy circuit hugs the coast for a while before turning inland to explore the Ballimore Estate

2. **Glenan Bay** 84
Follow the coast from Portavadie before climbing to an abandoned village in the woods

3. **The Stillaig Loop** 86
Discover the ancient and recent history of this secluded corner of the Cowal peninsula

4. **The Armchair and the Ark** 88
Discover two huge sculptures on the hillside above Tighnabruaich

5. **Bealach a' Chaisteil** 90
Follow the old route out of Tighnabruaich before dropping down to return via the Cowal Way

6. **Ardyne and the Chinese Ponds** 92
This woodland circuit visits two reservoirs modelled on traditional Chinese Willow Pattern crockery

7. **Bishop's Glen** 94
An easy loop of the reservoir at Bishop's Glen, near Dunoon, and the tumbling Balgaidh Burn which feeds it

Otter Ferry and the Ballimore Estate

Distance 3.6km **Time** 1 hour
Terrain mostly surfaced private roads; one short unsurfaced track
Map OS Explorer 362 **Access** bus to Otter Ferry from Largiemore and Tighnabruaich

At one time a bustling port where a ferry bypassed the long trip around the head of Loch Fyne, today Otter Ferry is a quiet community of scattered farms, fishermen's cottages and grander houses set along the shore of the loch.

The walk begins in the car park by the old stone jetty at Otter Ferry. The jetty was built by John Campbell of Otter, under instruction from the Commissioners of Supply. It was completed in 1773. The old ferry house, now a pub, sits behind the car park.

The ferry ran from Otter Ferry to West Otter Ferry on the opposite shore until the service ceased in the late 1940s. The fare in 1791 was 3d for a man and 9d for a horse, around a day's wages for a labourer at the time.

Keeping the sea on the right, walk down the private road which shortly leads south along the seafront. At low tide, a gravel spit can be seen stretching for over a mile into Loch Fyne. The name of the village is derived from the Gaelic for this spit, *An Oiter*, rather than from the native sea otters which scamper playfully around the rocky shores.

While it is certainly possible to walk along the spit, it is not recommended as the tide comes in quickly and can easily cut you off from dry land. The concrete structure by a sharp right angle in the road is the remains of a Second World War anti-submarine boom, from which point a net was stretched across the loch to West Otter Ferry.

Keep right at a fork to continue along the seafront, where the line of sycamore and oak trees above the retaining wall

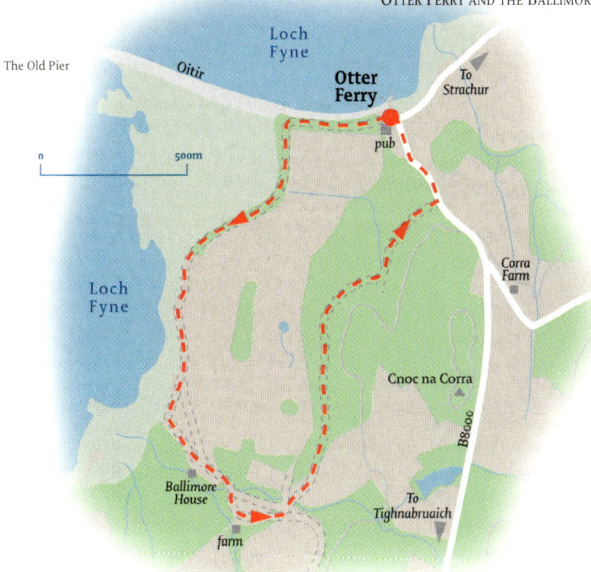

was planted in around 1820.

Pass several holiday lodges, before turning inland, where the road gives way to an unsurfaced vehicle track. Climb very gradually away from the sea to arrive at the impressive Ballimore House.

This mansion, originally named Otter House, was commissioned around 1832 by Mungo Nutter Campbell, a wealthy West Indies plantation owner, and designed and built by David Hamilton. The landscape around the house was laid out at around the same time and has changed little since then. The Campbells of Otter sold Otter House to Major MacRae-Gilstrap in 1899, and took the name with them to Achagoyle House near Kilfinan. Gilstrap renamed the estate Ballimore, and engaged William Leiper to enlarge the house in the Scottish Baronial style.

From the house, turn immediately left, then right to return to the road. Bear right at a junction to stay on the road, passing a farm and keeping left to go through a gate. Turn left at a junction and then immediately right at a fork, staying on the road and climbing very gradually through woodland of beech and sycamore, which was planted when the estate was built.

Keep straight ahead at the next junction to pass through the entrance to the Ballimore Estate. Turn left onto the main road, following it down the hill back to the beginning of the walk.

Glenan Bay

Distance 3.7km **Time** 1 hour 15
Terrain forest tracks, rocky shoreline
Map OS Explorer 362 **Access** bus to
Portavadie from Dunoon; ferry to
Portavadie from Tarbert

Trace this woodland circuit along the
shores of Loch Fyne before climbing to
reach an abandoned village. Although
this route may be walked at any time
of year, it is at its best in the spring,
when bluebells carpet the floor of the
ancient oakwood and the bracken is
not too high.

Portavadie, from the Gaelic *Port a'
Mhadaidh*, meaning the Port of Dogs (after
dog otters rather than the canine variety),
was built by the Scottish Office in the
1970s to construct concrete oil platforms
for the new North Sea Oil industry. The
complex was never used and it was
demolished in 1982.

Nevertheless, a ferry service between
Portavadie and Tarbert was established in
1994. The Loch Lomond and Cowal Way, a
long-distance walking trail which runs
from Portavadie to Inveruglas on Loch
Lomondside, was established in 2000. The
Portavadie Marina was opened in 2010 on
the site of the oil platform construction
complex, and now contains restaurants,
conference suites, retail and leisure space,
along with luxury accommodation.

The walk begins at the Glenan Wood car
park, on the northern side of the road and
250m along from the ferry terminal. Skip
around the gate at the far end of the car
park, quickly bearing left to cross a grassy
pasture. Entering woodland, wind down
to a rocky footpath by the shore.

Bear left, following the sign for the
Glenan Bay shore path, where an uneven
woodland track runs parallel to the shore,
dodging between large boulders, rocky

◀ Eilean na Beithe

outcrops, trees and bushes. Look out for Eilean na Beithe, an almost-island connected to the shore by a narrow isthmus.

Follow the path up and over a rocky outcrop before dropping down to reach Glenan Bay. This beach is a great spot to watch the ferry on its way to and from Tarbert. Continue along the track, quickly bearing right to climb a slope into the woodland. Turn left at the junction at the top to follow an undulating track through bracken and ancient oakwoods, rising to reach a junction 600m later. Bear left, dropping down to follow a burn. Cross it at a log bridge and climb the hill on the other side to reach the haunting remains of Glenan.

The village was first settled around 1309. Unlike many other Highland settlements, it survived the Clearances of the 18th and 19th centuries, and remained inhabited continuously until the early 20th century. Over 600 years, people who called Glenan home lived, worked, played and died here. According to local legend, the last inhabitant hung himself in the surrounding oakwoods rather than leave the village.

Having explored the village, go back down the hill and over the burn to return to the junction. Bear left for a gentle climb through woodland along an obvious track with occasional views across Loch Fyne to Knapdale on the opposite shore.

After 1.2km, emerge from the trees and turn right to follow a wider track between bracken and gorse. Cross a grassy pasture to meet with the outward track, turning left to return to the car park.

The Stillaig Loop

Distance 7km **Time** 2 hours
Terrain moorland track, unsurfaced vehicle track; mild ascent and descent
Map OS Explorer 362 **Access** bus to Portavadie from Dunoon; ferry from Tarbert

The landscape in this quiet corner of Cowal offers some of the most beautiful views in Scotland. People have made many attempts to live here and this route passes Bronze Age standing stones, an abandoned 19th-century farming settlement and the site of a long gone 20th-century village.

The route begins at the Glenan Wood car park. Return to the road and turn left, following it for 900m. Reaching a T-junction, turn right then almost immediately left. This was the former site of the ghost village of Pollphail.

In the 1970s, several locations around the coast of Scotland were chosen as construction sites to build platforms for the nascent North Sea Oil industry. One such site was at Portavadie, where a construction yard to construct deep water oil gravity platforms was built. Pollphail was built between 1975 and 1977 to provide accommodation for up to 500 workers for the new yard. Unsurprisingly, due to the distance from Portavadie to the North Sea, no orders were placed at the yard, and Pollphail was never occupied. The construction yard is now the site of Portavadie Marina. Pollphail fell into ruin, and was finally demolished in December 2016.

A marked path forks off on the right. Follow it as it winds through woodland, climbing steps uphill and catching brief views back to the marina.

Leave the woodland as the track levels out to cross heather moorland. Turn right

THE STILLAIG LOOP

◀ Cnoc Pollphail standing stone

at a junction, following the sign for the Stillaig Loop. Continue across a couple of boardwalks, following the obvious waymarked track.

Swing southwards to pass a large standing stone at Cnoc Pollphail. A smaller stump where another stone has been broken is nearby. The stones are thought to date from the Bronze Age.

Continue along the path, bearing left at a waymarker to cross another boardwalk. Look out for an old ruined building around 200m to the right. This is part of Low Stillaig. Unlike the 1970s' Pollphail, this abandoned 19th-century settlement is still standing. The building contains several unconnected rooms, and probably provided homes for farm labourers. Its construction date is not known, but it was occupied in 1863 when the first OS map of the area was published.

Cross another boardwalk, following the track down to cross a bridge over a burn. Continue across a wide, open green pasture, aiming for a gap in the wall at the opposite side. Where the path splits, bear left to join an unsurfaced vehicle track. Follow it past a wooden hut straight ahead, dropping down to reach a narrow isthmus. From here, the walk may be extended by crossing the narrow strip of land to explore Eilean Aoidhe if you wish.

Return past the hut, which is a sailing base for the Boys Brigade, and follow the vehicle track up the hill. Look out for the Creag Loisgte standing stone on the left.

The track winds across the moorland, climbing a hill to arrive at a gate. Beyond the gate, turn left to follow the road back down to the beginning of the walk.

The Armchair and the Ark

Distance 3.6km **Time** 1 hour 15 **Terrain** formal and informal roads, unsurfaced hill tracks; the climb to the Armchair is very steep and can be slippery in the wet **Map** OS Explorer 362 **Access** bus to Tighnabruaich from Dunoon and Portavadie

The village of Tighnabruaich nestles into the Cowal coastline, a long strip of houses and shops tucked into the narrow gap between the steep hillside and the Kyles of Bute. This route climbs to the summit of Dùn Mor, 164m above the village, where a huge wooden chair offers superb views, before investigating a wake-up call to climate change.

The walk begins in the Tighnabruaich car park, 200m northwest of the RNLI Lifeboat Station. Return to the shore road, turning left to wander along the waterfront. Around 300m from the car park, and about 140m before reaching the pier, turn up a steep single-track road on the left to climb up through the village in a couple of switchbacks. The road deteriorates into a vehicle track beyond the second bend.

Turn left at a junction, following a sign for the New Road. The vehicle track peters out altogether here, becoming an unsurfaced foot track which leads up the hill in an almost straight line to emerge at one end of a lay-by on the main road which leads down into Tighnabruaich.

This road, quiet and single-track for most of its length, is relatively new, dating only as far back as the 1960s, when it was constructed to connect Tighnabruaich to the rest of Cowal more readily than the old road (now the B8000) did. Prior to its construction, passengers

THE ARMCHAIR AND THE ARK

◀ The Tighnabruaich Ark

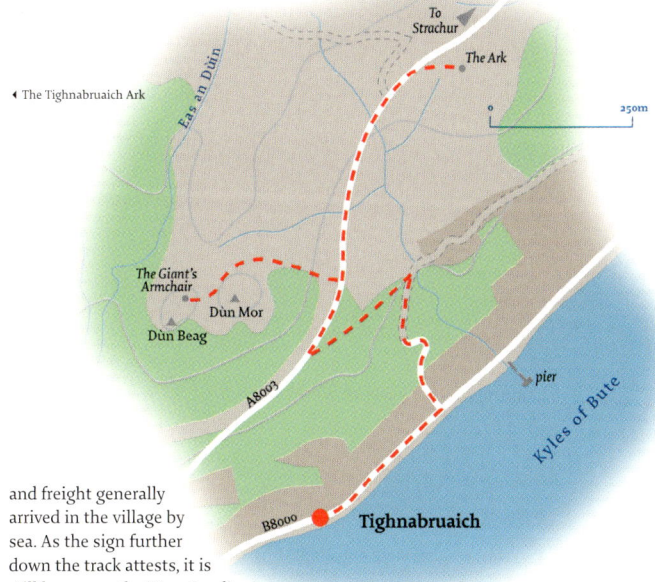

and freight generally arrived in the village by sea. As the sign further down the track attests, it is still known as the 'New Road'.

Turn right to walk to the far end of the lay-by and cross the road, where a wooden post marks steps which climb to a gate. Beyond the gate, continue very steeply uphill beside a fence. The track levels out as it begins to pull away from the fence, crossing almost flat heather-clad hillside to reach the Giant's Armchair.

Known locally simply as 'The Big Chair', this is exactly what it says it is: a huge wooden chair. Steps up one of the front legs allow you to clamber up to the platform to enjoy views across the Kyles of Bute to Bute itself.

Return down the hill to the road and turn left, striding uphill to the next lay-by, where a huge skeletal boat can be seen on the hillside. Go through a gate at the far end of the lay-by and follow the grassy track up to it.

This elegant structure is the Tighnabruaich Ark. It was built by local woodsman David Blair deliberately invoking the biblical story of Noah and the flood to draw a parallel with the impact of climate change on sea levels.

It was constructed using larch trees that were felled due to fungal disease and is over 20m long, 6m high and 5m wide, with a bench seat all the way round.

Retrace your steps back down the road to the beginning of the walk.

89

Bealach a' Chaisteil

Distance 6.8km **Time** 2 hours 15
Terrain roads, pavements, unsurfaced tracks; steep ascents **Map** OS Explorer 362
Access bus to Tighnabruaich from Dunoon and Portavadie

Follow this ancient route to the summit of Creag Rubha Bhàin, before returning along the seafront.

Until the end of the 19th century, the only route east out of Tighnabruaich was along the Bealach a' Chaisteil, the 'Pass of the Castle'. There are many 'Bealachs a' Chaisteil' throughout the Highlands. The term refers to any strategic point with a natural defence, in this case the rocky escarpment leading up to Creag Rubha Bhàin, which towers above the eastern end of the village and is topped by a transmitter mast. The route was superseded in 1897 when a footpath was created along the shore, which today forms part of the Cowal Way. The Bealach a' Chaisteil was recreated in 2003 by the Kilfinan Greenways Association, as part of a project to reinstate all the old paths alongside the North Kyle.

Beginning in Tighnabruaich car park, return to the seafront and turn left along the shore road, passing the pier. A pier was originally built here in 1843 by the Castle Steamship Company. Before this, Tighnabruaich did not exist. A stopping place for Clyde puffers and paddle steamers, the village grew up as a collection of villas for the wealthy of Glasgow to escape from the city. The pier was rebuilt in 1885. The sea remained Tighnabruaich's primary connection with the outside world until the A8003 was built in the 1960s.

Turn left up the next road, climbing

steeply and bearing right at a junction to continue straight ahead. Bear left as the road begins to curve back down the hill, following the sign for the 'New Road' to take an unsurfaced track, the Bealach a' Chaisteil, up through woodland. Keep left to follow a fence uphill, staying by the fence at the next junction. Hop over a burn, keeping left to leave the woodland.

As the track levels, turn right to cross a burn by a wooden bridge. After a couple more bridges, pass beneath a canopy of rhododendrons and begin to climb upwards again. The track curves to cross a bridge and meet with the access track for the transmitter mast which is perched on the summit of Creag Rubha Bhàin. The summit offers excellent views across the Kyles of Bute, with Bute itself obvious across the narrow straits. Dinghies and small yachts are scattered across the sea by Tighnabruaich, and the West Kyle stretches south towards the Isle of Arran.

Follow the access track back, climbing over a stile to arrive at the road into Tighnabruaich. Turn right, striding up the hill and turning right again after 400m, following the sign for the Shore Path. Here, a fairly steep unsurfaced path drops quickly downhill between a burn and a fence, opening out into a vehicle track by a couple of cottages.

Turn right at the bottom of the hill, joining the Cowal Way and heading back towards Tighnabruaich. This is the 1897 footpath. The track drops gently down towards the shore, becoming a formal road by the Tighnabruaich boatyard. Continue along the road to the start.

◀ The Kyles of Bute from Creag Rubha Bhàin

Ardyne and the Chinese Ponds

Distance 3.9km **Time** 1 hour 15
Terrain unsurfaced hill and forest tracks; moderate ascent, can be damp underfoot
Map OS Explorer OL37 **Access** no public transport to the start

In 1818, Kirkman Finlay, Lord Provost of Glasgow and head of Scotland's largest textile manufacturing business at the time, bought land on the lower slopes of the Cowal peninsula, facing Rothesay Bay, and built a mansion house, named Castle Toward after the nearby 15th-century Toward Castle. The land had previously belonged to the Campbells of Auchavoulin, and is alternatively known as the Auchavoulin Estate.

This trail follows sections of the Castle Toward Estate's original Victorian-era paths, climbing through young native woodland on the lower slopes of Buachailean and enjoying views over the Firth of Clyde to Bute and the Cumbraes. The route follows yellow waymarkers throughout. Look out for red squirrel and red deer among the trees.

The walk begins in the Ardyne Forestry Commission car park, off the A815 Glenstriven Road. Follow the rough track out of the far end of the car park, bearing left to cross a burn, before climbing uphill through woodland of silver birch.

After 400m, turn left at a junction to follow a long straight path up the hill, enjoying magnificent views across Loch Striven as you climb. During the Second World War, the loch was secretly used by a team of engineers led by Barnes Wallis to test the innovative Highball bomb, a precursor to the 'bouncing bombs' used in the famous Dambusters attacks on Germany in 1943.

By a waymarker, turn right to climb a steep grassy track which offers excellent views across to Bute. The silver birchwood is quickly replaced by conifers, and the path becomes boggy in places.

Reaching another junction, turn left,

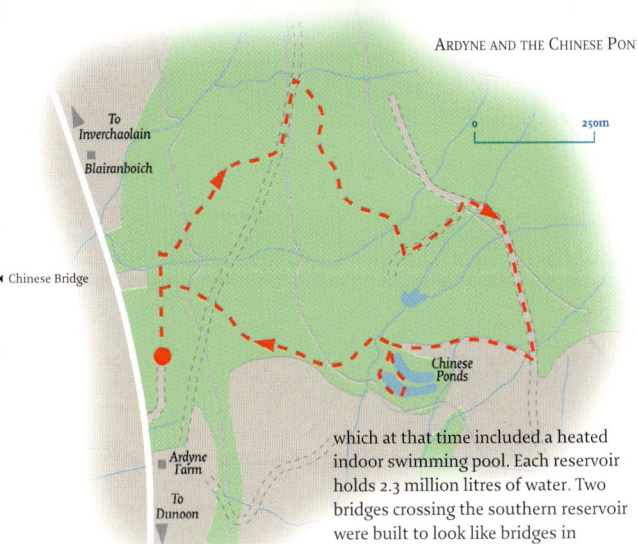

climbing a wide roughly cobbled track. At the top, turn right onto a broad vehicle track, following the sign for the Corlaroch Loop. Go right again by another waymarker to descend on an unsurfaced track.

Turn left at a further waymarker, passing a 'No Swimming' sign, and bearing left again to arrive at a small picturesque reservoir surrounded by reeds and rhododendrons. Turn right, passing between rhododendron bushes to cross a second reservoir by a small stone bridge.

Following Finlay's death in 1842, Castle Toward and the surrounding estate passed through various owners until 1919, when it was bought by Major Andrew Coats, a wealthy Paisley thread maker. Coats constructed these reservoirs to supply water to the Castle Toward Estate, which at that time included a heated indoor swimming pool. Each reservoir holds 2.3 million litres of water. Two bridges crossing the southern reservoir were built to look like bridges in traditional Chinese Willow Pattern crockery, and the reservoirs became known as the Chinese Ponds.

Continue straight ahead over the second bridge, and turn right to return to the main track. Carry on down the hill, bearing right to follow an aggregate path through silver birchwood.

The estate was requisitioned by the War Department during the Second World War, and, renamed *HMS Brontosaurus*, became No 2 Combined Training Centre, where officers and men of the Royal Navy, Army, RAF Regiment and ground crews were trained in preparation for raids and amphibious landings such as those at Dieppe, North Africa, Sicily, Salerno, Normandy and Walcheren.

At the bottom of the hill, turn left to follow the outward route back to the car park.

Bishop's Glen

Distance 3.2km **Time** 1 hour
Terrain good unsurfaced tracks
Map OS Explorer OL37 **Access** no public transport to the start; bus to Dunoon from Glasgow, Portavadie or Carrick Castle, or ferry to Dunoon from Gourock, a 1km walk from the start

At one time, Bishop's Glen, in the hills above Dunoon, was known simply as Balgaidh Glen, after the Balgaidh Burn, which ran through it. The first of the glen's three reservoirs was built in the 1870s and supplied water to Dunoon until the 1970s, when a pipeline was laid from Loch Eck. During this time, the area became known as the Waterworks, until it was renamed Bishop's Glen in a 1950s' tourist initiative, after nearby Bishop's Seat.

This pleasant, easy circuit explores the glen's last remaining reservoir and the Balgaidh Burn which feeds it. The network of paths around the glen are well-constructed and maintained, and are very straightforward to follow.

The glen is teeming with wildlife. If you visit in the evening, you may be rewarded with glimpses of roe deer and fox. As night falls, pipistrelle bats flit around the trees and tawny owls begin their hunt.

The route begins in the small visitors' car park at the top end of Dunoon's Nelson Street, where the road continues onwards into Bishop's Glen. Walk along the road, climbing gradually and passing a viewpoint where water from the reservoir gushes from an outlet.

Approaching the grass-covered wall of the dam, turn left to cross a bridge across the reservoir outlet before bearing right to climb to the reservoir itself.

The old reservoir is now enjoying a new lease of life as a premier fishing spot, and is regularly stocked with rainbow trout. Watch for the trout rising to snap at

◀ Bishop's Glen

insects. Herons stalk the shallows while gold-ringed dragonflies pursue midges and mosquitoes around the water's edge. Ducks are the most easily spotted birds on the reservoir but, if you are lucky, you might even spot the black plumage of a great cormorant. Buzzards soar high above, hunting for rabbits and other small mammals.

Follow the path for 200m, bearing right just before a gate to wander along a pleasant woodland path beside the reservoir banks. Look out for red squirrels scampering among the trees, and for treecreepers searching for insects up and down the tree trunks. You might also hear the loud drumming of a great spotted woodpecker.

Drop down some steps, continuing through the trees before turning left just before a river, the Balgaidh Burn, flows into the reservoir. The path follows an old broken-down fence up the glen for a little before dropping down to cross a bridge.

Turn left at a junction to amble high above the river which flows through a deep gorge beside the path. Walk down some steps on the right to cross a wide bridge over the river, following a wooden walkway back down the other side. The walkway gives way to an unsurfaced path, swinging away from the river and becoming an engaging woodland ramble.

Joining the reservoir again, head through a fishing car park, curving around the dam and turning left to follow the road back down to the beginning of the walk.

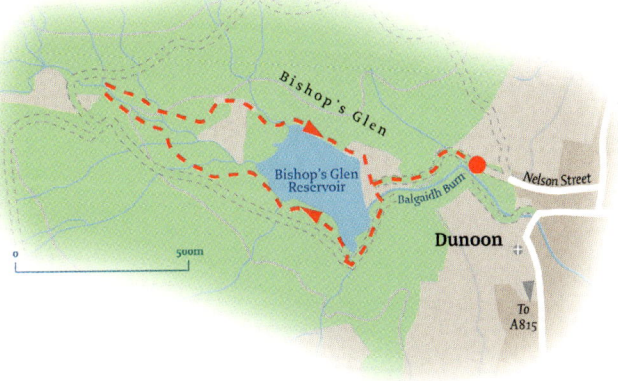

Index

Achamore Gardens	56	Glenan Bay	84
Ardminish	52, 54, 56	Glenramskill	44
Ardrishaig	16	Keil Caves	48
Ardyne	92	Kilbrannan Sound	30, 36
Arichonan	8	Kilchattan Bay	76, 78
Auchavoulin Estate	92	Kintyre Way, The	32, 44, 48
Ballimore Estate	82	Knapdale Forest	8
Balnakailly	64	Laggan, The	40
Barone Hill	74	Loch Barnluasgan	10
Bealach a' Chaisteil	90	Loch Caolisport	18
Beinn Ghuilean	40	Loch Coille-Bharr	12
Bishop's Glen	94	Loch Fyne	26, 82, 84
Bodach, The	60	Loch Gilp	16
Cailleach, The	60	Loch Linne	10
Cairn Bàn	66	Loch Sween	8
Campbeltown	40	Machrihanish	38
Campbeltown Loch	42	Mull of Kintyre, The	46
Canada Hill	72	Otter Ferry	82
Caol Scotnish	8	Pollphail	86
Carradale	34	Port Ban	24
Castle Toward	92	Port Bannatyne	70
Creag Bhàn	54	Portavadie	84, 86
Creag Rubha Bhàin	90	Rothesay	68, 70, 72, 74
Crinan Canal	16	Saddell Bay	36
Cruach an t-Sorchain	26	St Blane's Church	76, 78
Cruach Breacain	16	St Columba's Cave	18
Crucifixion Cave, The	42	Skipness	30
Cuddyport Beach	58	Southend	48
Davaar Island	42	Steallair Dubh, The	18
Deer Hill	32	Stillaig	86
Dunaverty Rock	48	Stravanan Bay	76
Dunoon	94	Tarbert	24, 26
Dùn a' Choin Duibh	20	Taynish	14
Dùn Mor	88	Tighnabruaich	88, 90
Dùn Skeig	28	Torinturk Forest	20
East Loch Tarbert	26	Tramway Trail, The	68
Ettrick Bay	68	West Island Way	68, 70, 76, 78
Gauldrons, The	38	West Loch Tarbert	28
Glean a' Gealbhan	8	White Shore, The	24